THE SEARCH FOR JESUS
MODERN SCHOLARSHIP LOOKS AT THE GOSPELS

■   ■   ■   ■   ■   ■

Symposium at the Smithsonian Institution
September 11, 1993

Sponsored by the Resident Associate Program

■   ■   ■

HERSHEL SHANKS, MODERATOR
STEPHEN J. PATTERSON
MARCUS J. BORG
JOHN DOMINIC CROSSAN

BIBLICAL ARCHAEOLOGY SOCIETY
Washington, DC

Designed by Auras Design, Washington, DC

Library of Congress Catalog Card Number: 94-70539
ISBN 1-880317-14-1 (paperbound)

©1994 Biblical Archaeology Society
4710 41st Street, NW
Washington, DC 20016

▪ CONTENTS ▪

▪ PARTICIPANTS ▪

HERSHEL SHANKS, moderator, is editor of *Biblical Archaeology Review* and *Bible Review.* He is also the editor and author of many books, including *Understanding the Dead Sea Scrolls* (Random House, 1992).

JOHN DOMINIC CROSSAN is professor of religious studies at DePaul University in Chicago. He was a founder of *Semeia: An Experimental Journal for Biblical Criticism* and general editor from 1980 to 1986. He was also a founder and co-director (with Robert W. Funk) of the Westar Institute Jesus Seminar from 1985 to 1993. His book *The Cross That Spoke: The Origins of the Passion Narrative* (Harper & Row, 1988) received the 1989 Award for Excellence in the Study of Religion (Analytical-Descriptive Studies) from the American Academy of Religion. Professor Crossan has just completed a trilogy on the historical Jesus: *The Historical Jesus: The Life of a Mediterranean Jewish Peasant* (1991); *Jesus: A Revolutionary Biography* (1993); and *The Essential Jesus: Original Sayings and Earliest Images* (1994), all published by HarperSanFrancisco.

STEPHEN J. PATTERSON has been assistant professor of New Testament studies at Eden Theological Seminary in Saint Louis since 1988. He specializes in the study of the historical Jesus, Christian origins and the Gospel of Thomas, an early Christian gospel not found in the New Testament. Professor Patterson is co-author of *The Q-Thomas Reader* (Polebridge, 1990; with John Kloppenborg, Marvin Meyer and Michael Steinhauser) and author of *The Gospel of Thomas and Jesus* (Polebridge, 1993). He is also a contributing editor to *Bible Review.*

MARCUS J. BORG is Hundere Distinguished Professor of Religion and Culture at Oregon State University, past chair of the Historical Jesus Section of the Society of Biblical Literature and a Fellow of the Jesus Seminar. He is the author of several books, including: *Conflict, Holiness and Politics in the Teachings of Jesus* (Edwin Mellen, 1984); *Jesus, A New Vision* (1987) and *Meeting Jesus Again for the First Time* (1994), both published by HarperSanFrancisco; and *Jesus in Contemporary Scholarship*, which will be published by Trinity Press International.

INTRODUCTION:
DEFINING THE PROBLEM

Our topic is one of the hottest buttons in biblical studies and is of enormous public interest. One sign of this public interest is that two books on the subject were recently reviewed on the front page of the *New York Times*. When was the last time you can remember a book being reviewed on the front page of the *New York Times?* One of those books was written by Dom Crossan, who is one of our lecturers.

We have given this symposium a rather exciting subtitle, "Modern Scholarship Looks at the Gospels." But scholars refer to the subject as historical Jesus studies. In short, what do modern historians say about the birth, life and death of Jesus?

Critical scholarship of the New Testament is barely 200 years old. The first book to deal with the New Testament in a critical scholarly way was published in 1778. It was written by a German scholar named Samuel Reimarus. Interestingly, it was not published until ten years after the author died, and even then, it was published anonymously. This gives you some idea of how dangerous it was to engage in this kind of inquiry at that time. The fears of the publisher and the author's family were not entirely unjustified. At about the same time, Thomas Paine's publisher in England went to jail for publishing *The Age of Reason*. And in 1697, an 18-year-old Scottish student was hanged for claiming that Ezra, rather than Moses, wrote the Pentateuch.

The most famous work in the history of historical Jesus studies is, of course, *The Quest of the Historical Jesus* by Albert Schweitzer, published in the early 20th century. And that really marks the second phase in historical Jesus studies. But scholars soon decided that Schweitzer had been unsuccessful in his quest and that the task was impossible. We could not know the historical Jesus.

After Schweitzer, there was a kind of hiatus on the subject. There are fads in scholarship just as there are in the width of men's ties. Probably mostly for theological reasons that we don't have the time to explore here, there was little interest in the quest for the historical Jesus once the second wave led by Schweitzer failed.

But in the last ten or twenty years, interest in this subject has burgeoned. That is why we are here today. We are now in the floodtide of the third phase of historical Jesus studies. One reason for the renaissance is that an enormous amount of new material is now available—archaeological finds, the Dead Sea Scrolls, the Nag Hammadi Codices, new perspectives on excavating literary texts and new anthropological perspectives concerning the social world in which Jesus lived.

Two aspects of our subject are especially sensitive, and I want to lay those on the table at the outset. We Americans are justly proud of our tolerance for ideas and beliefs that we may not share, but we don't discuss them much because they are not things you talk about in polite society. Today we are going to consider some controversial ideas in a scholarly way, and I want to address them frankly. The first is the factual historicity of the gospel accounts of Jesus' birth, life and death. Are there things in the gospels that scholars believe are historically inaccurate? The second sensitive issue is anti-Jewish, perhaps even anti-Semitic, passages in the New Testament. These, too, will be a concern, both explicitly and implicitly.

As to the first question—the factual historicity of the gospel accounts—we need to distinguish the Jesus of history from the Christ of faith. We are going to deal here with the former, not the latter. We are going to look at the gospel accounts objectively, as critical, modern historians.

There is, of course, another perfectly legitimate way of addressing these documents. Christians belong to a faith community, and faith, by definition, is not subject to objective scientific verification. Faith deals with ultimate questions, things that are beyond the testable, the empirical or the provable by reason. So we will not speak here of questions of faith. Those questions are for each of us to answer. Each of us must also decide how our faith intersects with what we judge to be the most likely historical scenario.

For many people, critical study of the New Testament deepens and enriches faith. Many even find it necessary because it reveals, in a new way, the human side of Jesus, which has been part of the faith of the Christian community since the very beginning.

A great Catholic scholar, Joseph Fitzmyer, has quoted *Time* magazine approvingly, and I'd like to quote it to you today. "The churches have always taught that Jesus Christ was a man as well as God, a man of a particular time and place, speaking a specific language, revealing his ways in terms of a specific cultural and religious tradition." That is our subject. And because of the terms of the discussion, because we will be looking at the evidence as objectively as possible, people of all faiths, or no faith, can participate. And that's one of the wonderful things about historical Jesus studies. It brings people together, regardless of their confessional perspective. Indeed, the various perspectives we bring to the task enrich the venture.

As for the gospel accounts, Fitzmyer also points out that there are three stages in the development of the gospel tradition. In stage one, we have what Jesus said and did in the first third of the first century. Stage two consists of what the disciples and the apostles taught and preached about what Jesus said and did. Stage three is the sequential narratives by the authors of the gospels, what they sifted out from the teachings of the disciples and apostles. Only stage three has been preserved. And this, in a sense, defines our problem. Starting from stage three, how do we get back to stage one, what Jesus said and did?

Today, three experts are going to lead us through the thickets of ancient texts, theology, archaeology, a little anthropology, the Nag Hammadi Codices and even the Dead Sea Scrolls. Our speakers are leading critical New Testament scholars who received their training at places as different as Harvard,

Oxford, the National University of Ireland and the Pontifical Biblical Institute. One of our speakers, Marcus Borg, is the outgoing chairman of the Historical Jesus Section of the Society of Biblical Literature. Another, Dom Crossan, is the incoming chairman of the Historical Jesus Section. This reflects their eminence in the field as well as the judgment of their colleagues as to their professional standing.

Our first speaker is Professor Stephen Patterson, who teaches New Testament at the Eden Theological Seminary in Saint Louis. Steve has a master's degree from Harvard and a doctorate from Claremont Graduate School in California. He is the author of *The Gospel of Thomas and Jesus* and co-author of *The Q-Thomas Reader*. He is a leading authority on Q, which, as you will hear in greater detail from him, is probably the earliest gospel and one that scholars are now excavating from ancient gospel texts.

Our second speaker is Marcus Borg, Hundere Distinguished Professor of Religion and Culture at Oregon State University. He received his doctorate from Oxford and did postgraduate studies at the University of Tübingen. His book *Jesus, A New Vision,* which has been enormously influential, has gone through five hardback printings and three paperback printings. Marcus also has two new books coming out—*Jesus in Contemporary Scholarship* and *Meeting Jesus Again for the First Time.* He is outgoing chairman of the Historical Jesus Section of the Society of Biblical Literature. Marcus is also a New Testament columnist for *Bible Review.*

Marcus' successor as chairman of the Historical Jesus Section of the Society of Biblical Literature is our third speaker, Professor John Dominic Crossan, professor of religious studies at DePaul University in Chicago. Professor Crossan was born in Ireland, as you will discover as soon as he opens his mouth. Dom received his doctorate from the National University of Ireland, and he has done postdoctoral studies at the Pontifical Biblical Institute in Rome and at the Ecole Biblique in Jerusalem. He is the author of 13 books, the most recent of which is *The Historical Jesus*, which was reviewed on the front page of the *New York Times*. For a previous book, *The Cross That Spoke: The Origins of the Passion Narrative*, Dom received the 1989 Award for Excellence in the Study of Religion from the American Academy of Religion. We could hardly have a more expert, diversified or exciting panel.

▪ STEPHEN J. PATTERSON ▪

I. SOURCES FOR A LIFE OF JESUS

There are many new things happening in gospel scholarship, including developments in literary criticism, studies grounded in sociology and anthropology, rhetorical criticism and the like. We will not be dealing with these developments, however. Rather, our topic is an older, more traditional one but still one of the most controversial, exciting and inescapable questions in the study of the New Testament. Who was Jesus, historically speaking? Historians work with sources, and I want to introduce you to the sources scholars use in addressing this question. But that is perhaps the most problematic part of the task, as you will soon see.

The Historians. Jesus came of age and spent his brief career under the reign of Tiberius Caesar, who succeeded Augustus in the year 14 and ruled until 37, well after Jesus' execution. Our most thorough Roman historian of this time, Tacitus, wrote of this period: "Sub Tiberio quies" (Under Tiberius, nothing happened) *(History* 5.9). This illustrates a problem. Jesus was an obscure figure in a remote part of the world, a speck on the wing of history. For centuries he would go unnoticed and remain unknown. Outside of Christian circles, almost no one took note of his life or death. Almost...but we do have a few brief notices.

Speaking of Christians, Tacitus (56 C.E.-c. 117 C.E.) writes in his *Annals* (15.44):

> The founder of this sect, Christus, was given the death penalty in the reign of Tiberius by the procurator, Pontius Pilate; suppressed for the moment, the detestable superstition broke out again, not only in Judea where the evil originated, but also in [Rome], where everything horrible and shameful flows and grows.

So much for making a good impression on Rome.

A second notice is found in the works of the great Jewish historian, Josephus (37 C.E.-c. 100 C.E.). Josephus is more complimentary of his Jewish countryman but not as complimentary as the Christian monastics who preserved the manuscripts of Josephus would have us believe. When reading Josephus, one must always be wary of the presence of interpolations added by Christian scribes to bring this important voice to bear witness to the Christian gospel. In the following quotation from Josephus' *Antiquities of the Jews* I have indicated in italics those places where scholars agree that a Christian hand has intruded:

About this time there lived Jesus, a wise man, *if indeed one ought to call him a man.* For he was one who wrought surprising feats and was a teacher of such people as accept the truth gladly. He won over many Jews and many of the Greeks. *He was the messiah.* When Pilate, upon hearing him accused by men of the highest standing among us, had condemned him to be crucified, those who had in the first place come to love him did not give up their affection for him. *On the third day he appeared to them restored to life, for the prophets of God had prophesied these and countless other marvelous things about him.* And the tribe of Christians, so called after him, has still to this day not disappeared.

Antiquities of the Jews 18.63

So much for the historians. All told, they tell us little.

Other Jewish References. But there are other Jewish references to Jesus indicating that he did not go entirely unnoticed among his people. One of the most important is this one from the Babylonian Talmud (c. 500/600 C.E.):

On the eve of Passover they hanged Yeshu [of Nazareth] and the herald went before him 40 days saying, "[Yeshu of Nazareth] is going forth to be stoned, since he practiced sorcery and cheated and led his people astray. Let everyone knowing anything in his defense come and plead for him." But they found nothing in his defense and hanged him on the eve of Passover.

BT *Sanhedrin* 43a

Then, a little later the same text continues:

Jesus had five disciples: Mattai, Maqai, Metser, Buni, and Todah.

BT *Sanhedrin* 43a

Not the traditional 12, but interesting nonetheless.

Still, all of these sources tell us precious little about the historical Jesus. All we learn from them is that he was a Jewish teacher of wisdom with a reputation for sorcery who had a few disciples and, perhaps, a somewhat larger following who, after his execution at the hands of Roman authorities, did not entirely give up on him. For some, that much is enough. Those who want more must turn to the documents produced by those unflappable hangers-on—in the words of Josephus—that "tribe of Christians."

Paul. Of that tribe, the first person who left behind anything in writing was Paul of Tarsus. But in all of his letters, Paul never speaks of Jesus' life. Paul rarely even refers to anything Jesus said during his lifetime. This is understandable because Paul never knew Jesus personally. Paul became part of the following of Jesus only after Jesus had been crucified. His experience of Jesus was limited to spiritual experiences, which he understood to be "revelation" from Jesus Christ, whom he believed God had raised from the dead (Galatians 1:11-17). In terms of history, then, Paul is a wash. For anything about Jesus' life, we must wait several years for the writing of the first gospels.

The Synoptic Problem. There are four Gospels in the New Testament: Matthew, Mark, Luke and John. The last of these, John, is, for complex reasons, of little value to the historian. John's view of Jesus is quite different from the others, both in terms of the events described and the message Jesus preaches. Since the 19th century, scholars have regarded John as a spiritual reflection on Jesus with loose connections to the historical person. Today, many regard John as a quasi-Gnostic interpretation of Jesus. In any event, John seldom comes into the current discussion.

The other three Gospels, Matthew, Mark and Luke, are closely related. Since the 18th century, scholars have noticed that they share a common view of Jesus' ministry—we call them the Synoptic Gospels, from the Greek word meaning "seeing together."[1]

In 1776, Johann-Jakob Griesbach[2] noticed that, with respect to the biographical outline of Jesus' life, Matthew and Luke agree only when they also agree with Mark. Griesbach explained this by suggesting that Matthew wrote his Gospel first. Then Luke wrote, using Matthew loosely. Finally, Mark wrote his Gospel, combining Matthew and Luke but only using those things which they both share.

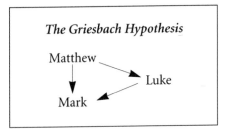

The Griesbach Hypothesis

Matthew

Mark   Luke

For 50 years this hypothesis held sway—and in a few circles it is still preferred today.[3] But a majority of scholars began to feel dissatisfied with it because it simply did not account for the evidence, even on its own terms. For example, both Matthew and Luke begin with accounts of Jesus' birth and end with his resurrection (hardly inconsequential matters)—but Mark includes neither of these. Perhaps more astonishing, however, both Matthew and Luke agree in opening Jesus' ministry with the Sermon on the Mount (or Plain in Luke); but Mark says nothing about it. Scholars also began to notice that Mark's Greek was much less polished than Matthew's and especially Luke's. Could one imagine Mark ruining the perfectly good prose of his predecessors?

To account for these and a myriad of similar, though less obvious, problems, C. H. Weisse, H. J. Holtzmann, J. Weiss and other 19th-century scholars proposed another hypothesis.[4] Rather than Matthew, they said, *Mark* wrote first. Then, Matthew and Luke wrote independently of one another, each using Mark as a source. That would explain why Matthew and Luke agree in terms of the general outline only when they also agree with Mark. They both used Mark as a source. This is called the hypothesis of Markan priority.

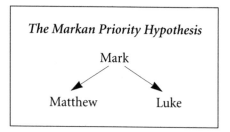

The Markan Priority Hypothesis

Mark

Matthew   Luke

But there were still problems. The most pressing was the large amount of material shared by Matthew and Luke but not found in Mark. This material was most intriguing. In it there is a high degree of verbal agreement between Matthew and Luke. And it is presented in more or less the same order. However, they almost always insert it differently into Mark's outline. It is as though they shared a list of sayings, parables and the like but no blueprint for where these things should go in the life of Jesus.

Based on these observations, Weisse, Holtzmann, Weiss and others proposed a second hypothesis. In addition to Mark, which provided the basic outline for a life of Jesus, they said, Matthew and Luke had a second source consisting primarily of sayings and parables. Because this source did not survive the ancient period, Weisse simply called it the "Source," *Quelle* in German. Later this was shortened to the simple siglum, Q. Thus was born the two-source hypothesis, that is, that Matthew and Luke had two sources, Mark and a second source, now lost, which we call Q. Because it did not survive, this second source, Q, must be reconstructed rather imperfectly by extracting it from Matthew and Luke.

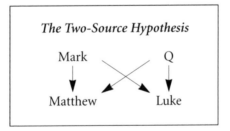

We will return to Q shortly, but for now I want to focus on Mark because Mark is our first narrative gospel, the first to present us with what at least appears to be part of Jesus' life.

Mark. If we are to assess Mark as a source for historical research, we must first ask what sort of document it is. We call it a gospel, but this tells us little. On the one hand, so many different documents are called gospels in antiquity it is almost impossible to define just what is meant by the term. On the other hand, Mark and the other books we now call gospels were not originally called gospels. Originally they bore only an ascription.

Marcion, an unorthodox Christian teacher active in the second century, is probably the first to have used this term with regard to one of the Gospels. He applied it to Luke—specifically to Luke and not the others. In Marcion's view, only Luke got it right, along with Paul. Marcion rejected the Hebrew Scriptures and most early Christian writings as too Jewish. Luke alone was "good news," i.e., *gospel*—in Greek, *euaggelion*, which literally means "good news." Eventually most Christians rejected Marcion's views, asserting that Matthew, Mark and John were also good news, and so they also came to be called gospels. But none of this tells us what these books were like originally—or how and why they were written. For this we must turn to ancient sources and modern study. First to the ancient sources.

We are fortunate to have at least one ancient account of the making of a gospel, and it happens to be Mark. It comes to us rather indirectly from a certain elder who is claimed to have known Mark. His remarks are preserved in Eusebius, the fourth-century church historian, who got them from Papias, a church elder who lived around the turn of the first century; Papias, in turn, got them from an elder who knew Mark. Now, historians—even biblical historians—are not usually inclined to trust thirdhand accounts. Nonetheless, this little fragment is worth our attention because it illustrates how ancient Christians thought about these texts and challenges the assumptions moderns often bring to them. Papias' brief account reads as follows:

> And the presbyter used to say this, Mark became Peter's interpreter and wrote accurately all that he remembered, not indeed in the order in which things were said and done by the Lord. For he had not heard the Lord, nor had he followed him, but as I said, later on followed Peter, who used to give instruction as necessity demanded, but not making as it were an arrangement of the Lord's sayings, so that Mark did nothing wrong in thus writing down single points as he remembered them. For to one thing he gave attention, to leave out nothing of what he had heard and to make no false statements in them.
>
> Eusebius, *Ecclesiastical History* 3.39.15

Now from the modern point of view, what is intriguing about this account is that, on the one hand, it plainly says that Mark did not write things down in the right order—that is, he did not write an historically accurate life of Jesus. He simply did not have the necessary information to do so. But on the other hand, he seems to insist that Mark wrote things down accurately and made no false statements. When many people read this passage, they typically hear the last part—about Mark being accurate. They like that; it gives them a sense of security that in our culture only historical accuracy can bring. But when their attention is directed to the first part—about Mark not writing things down in the right order—then things get interesting! For a modern person reading Mark, it reads for all the world like a short biography. How could Mark write a biography in which the events or sayings were not in the right order and still claim accuracy? The explanation is not difficult, but for the historian it spells trouble.

First of all we must realize that there is nothing in antiquity that even roughly approximates our concept of historical biography. Classics, like Plutarch's *Lives*, are not easily transported into our world. These are not biographies, but aretalogies, that is, works whose purpose is to recount the wondrous deeds of great persons. Their purpose is not historical but doxological. This is true of Mark as well.

We did not need Papias' elder to tell us this. Since the end of the 19th century, when Martin Kaehler demonstrated that the Gospel of Mark could not be used to reconstruct the life of Jesus because it is a work of theology and not history, historians have approached Mark with caution.[5] The 20th century has brought even greater refinement to our understanding of exactly what Mark was doing with his writing. William Wrede suggests that Mark's task was really apologetical, that Mark wrote to explain that Jesus was not better known as the Messiah because he kept his true identity a secret.[6] Thus Jesus is always silencing people he cures or demons he casts out. Today Wrede's theory of the Markan Messianic Secret has been replaced by more sophisticated literary analyses.

Suffice it to say here that Mark was not an historian but, rather, a theologian. Mark writes, in his own words, the "good news" of Jesus Christ and not the bare facts of his life. For the historian, this is not good news. It means that Mark can be of little value in reconstructing the life of Jesus. But this has implications for Matthew and Luke as well, who both used Mark as a source for their "lives" of Jesus. This means that we really have no historical source, no historical record of Jesus' life. Beyond a few details—Jesus' origins in Galilee, his end in Jerusalem—precious little is known.

So how then can Papias' elder claim that Mark was nonetheless accurate? Accuracy is not an absolute concept but a relative one. Accuracy in achieving a goal depends on what one is trying to achieve. We tend to associate accuracy in a literary milieu with verbatim, objective accuracy. We can expect that kind of accuracy because it is achievable—with writing, recording devices, computers and the like. But this was not the case in antiquity.

In Mark's cultural milieu, only about five percent of people could read or write. People operated orally. No thought was given to writing things down. This was simply not part of most people's reality. Ninety-five percent of the people never wrote or read anything.[7] In such a milieu, accuracy means something quite different. In a culture that is primarily oral, verbatim accuracy is not achievable for most people, so most people never tried to achieve it. In fact, it barely existed as a concept in antiquity. The famous studies of oral cultures by Albert Lord in rural Yugoslavia showed that oral tradition is never repeated with verbatim accuracy, even though the bards charged with preserving these traditions claim vociferously that they are indeed rendered accurately.[8] With no texts around to define what accuracy means, it can and does mean something else altogether. To Lord's poets, it meant something like faithfulness to the tradition. To Mark and other early Christians, it probably meant something similar. This is fine for theologians; but for historians, these findings are ominous.

Methods. Let me assure you, however, that all is not lost—not yet. But we do need to recognize that when we look to these ancient texts, the gospels, for objective historical information, we are looking for something that was of little interest to the authors and may not even have existed as a concept in their world. Nonetheless, history *is* an important category in *our* world; and we are entitled to ask questions important to *us*. But we may need to develop special techniques for answering these questions, techniques and methods that respect the sources for what they are and not what we wish they were.

Multiple Attestation. Even if it is true that Mark's narrative—and, by implication, those of Matthew and Luke—is the product of the author's creativity and imaginative theological mind, this is not necessarily true of everything he includes in his narrative. The gospel writers lived in a world that was primarily oral. Their ability to read and write places them among the elite few who had access to literacy. Most people relied upon oral tradition. In fact, most people preferred it. They were suspicious of written words, words detached from someone who could take responsibility for them and shape them into a form appropriate to a given situation. Early Christians cultivated a lively oral tradition around Jesus. Most scholars believe that much, if not most, of the information collected in the gospels originally came from oral tradition. The question is how we can know for sure in individual cases.

One way is to look for traditions in more than one written source. When it seems certain that one of these sources did not make use of the other, we may assume that both sources derived from the common stock of early Christian oral tradition about Jesus. In other words, if two authors know the same story but do not know each other, we know that neither has created the story. Rather, a source must be assumed. Occasionally, as in the case of Q, a written source may be presumed. Usually, however, all we can assume is that both authors drew on a common oral tradition.

Until recently, multiple attestation had very limited value. Occasionally one might find a tradition attested independently in both Mark and John. One could also point to a handful of cases in which both Mark and Q seem to have a common tradition. But such cases were relatively few. For the most part, we simply had to assume that the gospel writers relied upon earlier oral traditions without being able to prove it.

That changed in 1945. In that year a remarkable library of books was discovered in the desert sands of Egypt. This collection is known as the Nag Hammadi Library, after the place of discovery, Nag Hammadi in Upper Egypt. Among the 50 or so tractates found at Nag Hammadi was a copy of the Gospel of Thomas. Scholars had known of the Gospel of Thomas through references to it in various early Christian authors. But no copy of it was known to have survived, that is until 1945, or rather 1957, when this text was finally published and made available to scholars for study.

There is much to say about Thomas, but let me cut to the chase for our purposes here. Two things about Thomas make it important to historical research about Jesus. First, of the 114 sayings and parables that make up the Gospel of Thomas, roughly half of them have parallels in the Synoptic Gospels. Therefore, if it should turn out that Thomas did not have direct knowledge of those Gospels or their sources, the amount of multiply attested material would be increased roughly 500 to 1,000 percent.

And that is the second thing. Careful study has shown that this is indeed the case. Thomas did not know the Synoptic

Gospels or their sources. It is, indeed, an independent witness to the Jesus tradition. We know this because, unlike Matthew and Luke relative to Q or Matthew and Luke relative to Mark, Thomas does not share with the Synoptic Gospels the things that tipped us off to the literary relationship that ties the Synoptics together. That is, there is no appreciable verbatim agreement between Thomas and the Synoptics; nor is there any shared order in the sequence in which material is presented.[9]

Now, what does multiple attestation tell us? It does not guarantee that a saying or story is historically accurate. It only tells us that an author did not create it from whole cloth.

But it may tell us something else as well. Dating the independent witnesses to a tradition gives us a limit, a date, before which that tradition must have existed. Now, scholars, by consensus, normally date Mark to around the year 70 C.E., that is, roughly contemporaneous with the Jewish war for independence from Rome. Q, which makes no reference to that catastrophic event, is normally dated 10 to 20 years earlier. Thomas is more difficult to date, but because it does not mention the Jewish war, I have argued that an initial Thomas collection may have existed prior to the war as well. This argument is reinforced by the observation that Q and Thomas are the same sort of gospel. Unlike the more familiar narrative gospels, Q and Thomas are simply collections of sayings and occasional brief stories. They belong to the earliest efforts of Christians to use literacy to transmit and use their oral traditions.

All this means that material that is attested in both Q and Thomas, or Mark and Thomas, or Mark and Q, or, on rare occasions, in Q, Mark and Thomas, forms the earliest verifiable layer of Christian tradition about Jesus. Professor Crossan has argued, and I would concur, that any historical treatment of Jesus should at least begin here.[10] This does not automatically exclude all other material in the rich and varied Jesus tradition, which by caprice might have been overlooked or dropped from one or more of these early sources. But it does provide a stable starting point.

Other Criteria. Now, just as this first stratum of material may not contain everything that the historian might trace to Jesus, neither should everything in this first stratum automatically be given positive historical evaluation. After all, material created or attributed to Jesus shortly after his death may have found its way into various gospels very early on. Thus, while multiple attestation gives us a rough starting point, we need to use other criteria for evaluating the Jesus tradition as well.

Kerygmatic Criterion. First, we must remember that the people who preserved and cultivated the Jesus tradition were not neutral. They had no objective historical interest. They cultivated the Jesus tradition because they believed that Jesus was special. To some, he was an envoy of God or God's agent, Sophia. To others, he was the Son of Man from Jewish apocalyptic lore. To others, he was the Son of God. To others, he was the Messiah, the Christ. The followers of Jesus made use of the traditions about Jesus and created new traditions to help them express their various convictions about Jesus. So, when evaluating traditional material, the first thing scholars look for is evidence of the influence of early Christian preaching about Jesus. What early Christians said about Jesus must be distinguished from things Jesus might plausibly have said about himself.

Scholars often refer to early Christian preaching as kerygma; accordingly, we might refer to this as the *kerygmatic criterion.*

Criterion of Social Formation. But theology was not the only thing early followers of Jesus were interested in. They also were engaged in organizing themselves and deciding on various social arrangements that would define who they were and how their group might continue. In Jesus' brief ministry, there is no evidence that he intended to form a church. Therefore, when evaluating the tradition, scholars also try to identify material reflecting the more elaborate processes of social formation that went on in the early church but not in the historical career of Jesus himself. Scholars sometimes refer to this as the *criterion of social formation.*

Criterion of Distinctiveness. Then there is the simple problem that Jesus became for early Christians a symbol of authority. Thus, Christians tended to attribute to him anything that functioned authoritatively for them. This included many popular aphorisms and common wisdom. The phenomenon may be illustrated with a modern analogy. How many people blithely assume that the very American, very modern, aphorism, "God helps those who help themselves," comes from the Bible? It does not. But to many modern Americans, the Bible symbolizes authority, especially in religious matters. Thus, when confronted with a saying mentioning God with the ring of authority, many people just naturally assume that it comes from the Bible. Early Christians, most of whom could not read or write, had no Bible, no texts at all. Rather, they had oral familiarity with a variety of wise sayings of various provenance, traditions, both sacred and secular, Jewish and pagan, all of which were considered, at a popular level, to carry some authority. They attributed many such things to Jesus, even though he may not have said them all, because he became for them a figure of great authority.

The Golden Rule is a good example of this. If Jesus did not say it, he is probably the only sage in antiquity who did not. But for just this reason, early Christians would have assumed Jesus said it even if he did not. Most of this material is not used by historians to reconstruct Jesus' preaching because it is not distinctive enough to be associated uniquely with any individual person. We call this the *criterion of distinctiveness.*

Coherence and the Environmental Criterion. Finally, there is an important rule that all historians must observe in this sort of speculative reconstructive work. The resulting picture must make some sense. This means that the material one regards as historical must form a reasonably coherent whole. This is the *criterion of coherence.* It also means that historical material must have some degree of plausibility given what we know about the religious and cultural world of the Mediterranean basin in the first century. This is sometimes referred to as the *environmental criterion.*

The Present Discussion in Scholarly Perspective. Enough of matters concerning method. I am eager to give way to my colleagues on the program today, Marcus Borg and John Dominic Crossan. Their important and creative historical work is part of a renaissance of interest in the historical Jesus, a movement that began in the early 1980s and is just now reaching its stride. The

British scholar Tom Wright has called this new impetus the third quest for the historical Jesus.[11] This, of course, implies that our work has been preceded by a "first quest" and a "second." Indeed, the quest for the historical Jesus is one of the oldest and most controversial topics in the history of New Testament scholarship. And so, a word or two to put the present work in perspective.

The first quest was carried on in Europe in the 19th century. The purpose was to apply the standards of reason and rational thought to the Gospels in order to arrive at a reasonable portrait of Jesus' life.[12] It assumed that the Gospel writers were attempting to write a history of Jesus' life, but that they were just too naive, superstitious or swayed by doctrinal concerns to do it. Reason, it was thought, could undo all their naiveté, superstition and piety. The first quest ran aground when it was realized that the Gospel writers were not naive historians but skilled theologians, preachers if you will, who expressed themselves in a religious idiom. When you remove the religious element from these texts using modern rationality, there is nothing left. The first quest died out for lack of material.

The second quest for the historical Jesus, referred to in the literature as the new quest, began in the 1950s and involved mostly German and American scholars.[13] They began with the proposition that the Gospels were not history but theology. But, they argued, it is possible that bits of history had been preserved through the oral tradition and taken up into the Gospels. Some of the methods I outlined today were developed by the new questers to recover those historical reminiscences. But ultimately their program was theological, not historical.

The new questers wanted to know if the preaching of the early church, which ultimately produced the Gospels, was in any way anticipated in Jesus' own preaching. The new quest lasted about ten years and died out for lack of interest. At the time other methods of biblical interpretation, especially literary criticism, commanded more interest and energy. There were also other ways of pursuing theology. The new questers were trying to write a history of theology, but few people were interested.

The third quest began in the early 1980s and includes titles by scholars from Britain, the Continent and North and South America. It is very diverse. The only thing that unites practitioners is historical interest. Their methods are varied, but most presume the basic methodological outline I have presented to you. They bring to the task greater knowledge of the ancient world than ever before and input from other fields of study, such as sociology, anthropology and linguistics. They tend also to be less centered on Jesus' preaching, a focus that united the new questers, and more attentive to things Jesus is said to have done, such as overturning tables in the Temple, or typical things, such as Jesus' practice of open-table fellowship.

Professors Crossan and Borg have been at the center of this new discussion; each will provide a glimpse of what it holds for us. But this new discussion is still too young for proper assessment. You are here to learn about work in progress. Where it will go historically, culturally and theologically is not yet known. Nor is it known if it is headed for as yet unseen shoals of disaster. All that can be said at this point is that the resurgence of interest, both lay and scholarly, has shown that, for some reason, history still matters in the postmodern world, and the Jesus of history may still make a difference.

ENDNOTES

1. These relationships may be seen in any number of synopses of the Gospels, reference tools in which parallel texts of the Gospels are placed in adjacent columns. A convenient English language synopsis is that of Burton H. Throckmorton, *Gospel Parallels* (Toronto: Thomas Nelson, 1967).

2. Griesbach introduced his theory in one of the earliest Gospel synopses, which he published in Latin: *Synopsis evangeliorum Matthaei, Marci, et Lucae* (Halle, 1776). He later published his conclusions in a book entitled *Commentatio qua Marci evangelium totum e Matthaei et Lucae commentariis decerptum esse monstratur* (Demonstration in which the entire Gospel of Mark is shown to be excerpted from the memoirs of Matthew and Luke) (Jena, 1789-90). This work was recently translated into English in Bernard B. Orchard and Thomas Longstaff, eds., *J. J. Griesbach: Synoptic and Critical Studies 1776-1976* (Cambridge, UK/New York: Cambridge University Press, 1978), see pp. 74-135.

3. In recent years this hypothesis has been revived by William Farmer and a number of his students. For a critical appraisal, see Christopher M. Tuckett, *The Revival of the Griesbach Hypothesis* (Cambridge, UK/New York: Cambridge University Press, 1983).

4. Christian Hermann Weisse, *Die evangelische Geschichte kritisch und philosophisch bearbeitet*, 2 vols. (Leipzig: Breitkopf und Hartel, 1838); Heinrich Julius Holtzmann, *Die synoptischen Evangelien* (Leipzig: Wilhelm Engelmann, 1863); Johannes Weiss, *Jesus' Proclamation of the Kingdom of God* (Philadelphia: Fortress, 1972). German original published in 1892.

5. Kaehler's work, published originally in German in 1896, is available in English: *The So-Called Historical Jesus and the Historic, Biblical Christ* (Philadelphia: Fortress, 1964).

6. William Wrede's work, published originally in German in 1901, is available in English: *The Messianic Secret* (Cambridge, UK: J. Clarke, 1971).

7. These figures are from William V. Harris, *Ancient Literacy* (Cambridge, MA: Harvard University Press, 1989).

8. Albert Lord, *The Singer of Tales* (Cambridge, MA: Harvard University Press, 1960). For a recent assessment, see Walter Ong, *Orality and Literacy* (New York: Methuen, 1982).

9. The relationship between Thomas and the Synoptic Gospels is, understandably, a hotly debated topic. The views presented here are my own, and they are argued in full in my book *The Gospel of Thomas and Jesus* (Sonoma, CA: Polebridge, 1993). North American scholars have tended to embrace this position; European scholars have tended to view Thomas as dependent upon the Synoptic Gospels.

10. John Dominic Crossan, *The Historical Jesus: The Life of a Mediterranean Jewish Peasant* (HarperSanFrancisco, 1992).

11. Stephen Niell and Tom Wright, *The Interpretation of the New Testament, 1861-1986*, 2d ed. (New York: Oxford University Press, 1988), p. 379.

12. The first quest was chronicled in one of the classic works of New Testament scholarship, Albert Schweitzer's *The Quest of the Historical Jesus* (New York: Macmillan, 1961).

13. The second or new quest was chronicled by James M. Robinson in *A New Quest of the Historical Jesus* (Philadelphia: Fortress, 1983).

QUESTIONS & ANSWERS

Could you comment on some of the popular books such as the Q book by Burton Mack, A. N. Wilson's biography of Jesus, Steven Mitchell's Gospel of Jesus?

The only one of those I can speak about out of intimate familiarity is Burton Mack's new book on Q, *The Lost Gospel* (HarperSanFrancisco, 1993). This is a very fine and exciting book. As a scholar, I would challenge him on a number of points, especially on the methods he uses. But in many important respects he is, in my view, quite right, even though he doesn't prove his point the way I would like him to. Burton Mack is a scholar of the highest standing, and I would take anything he says with utmost seriousness.

As for the books by Wilson (*Jesus* [Sinclair-Stephenson, 1992]) and Mitchell (*The Gospel according to Jesus* [HarperCollins, 1991]), I can only tactfully refer you to reviews in the literature. Mitchell's book, while creative, is not a work grounded in biblical scholarship. The quest for the historical Jesus is one of the most difficult projects in biblical scholarship. Unless you pay strict attention to a rigorous method, it is easy to end up saying almost anything you want about Jesus. The results can be exciting, but they reflect the views of the writer more than of Jesus. Some would argue that all Jesus scholarship suffers from such tendencies. That is the problem with working on a powerfully authoritative figure like Jesus. The temptation to place one's own views on his lips is great indeed. I recommend the recent books by those who share the podium with me today, Dom Crossan and Marcus Borg, as two that reflect such methodological rigor.

Why do you think Jesus did not write his own gospel?

Most scholars assume that Jesus did not read or write. In this respect Jesus was like most people of his day. Most people in antiquity did not read or write. *Ancient Literacy* (Harvard, 1989), a recent study by William Harris, shows that roughly 95 percent of people in the first century were illiterate. If you could read or write, you belonged to the very upper stratum of educated society. It is not likely that Jesus, who by all accounts was a peasant, or his early followers, likewise peasants, had access to that tool. Most important, people did not presume that in order to be remembered you had to write something. Most culture was transmitted orally. For that time and place it is not at all unusual that Jesus wrote nothing and that Christian traditions about Jesus were cultivated first by word of mouth.

This is unfortunate for us because we would prefer a written record; we trust books more than storytellers. But that was not so in antiquity. Many ancients didn't really trust the written word. They preferred the orally delivered word. Plato, for example, was rather suspicious of books. Papias, the early Christian elder upon whom we must rely for much of our information about earliest Christianity, was also distrustful of books, preferring instead to take his information from wandering apostolic descendants still active in his day. So we do not have a gospel from Jesus because he could not, and perhaps did not want to, write things down.

Oral traditions are very reliable; they don't change once they're established or become part of a ritual. How do we know that Q was not an oral tradition?

We know that Q was a written document because Matthew and Luke often have a high degree of verbal agreement in the passages they share. They also tend to present them in the same order, even though they may place them differently in Mark's outline, which they also used. These two elements—verbatim agreement and a common order—are what indicate Matthew and Luke used a common *written* source, not just a common oral tradition.

Much has been said over the years about the accuracy of oral tradition and whether or not oral traditions might be as accurate as written traditions. Some of this was in reaction to modern biblical scholars who came to negative conclusions about the historical accuracy of the Gospels. From my remarks today, you know where I stand on this issue.

For me one of the most important studies was Albert Lord's famous study from the 1950s, *The Singer of Tales* (see endnote 8, p. 28). Lord interviewed many bards from central Yugoslavia, who were said to have committed to memory long tales and ballads, some of them hundreds of lines in length, that had been passed down for centuries. When Lord asked the bards if they were repeating the songs verbatim, exactly as they had always been repeated, they said "Yes, of course we are." But when he recorded them and actually compared different performances of the same songs, he found that they were not repeating them verbatim. In fact, from one performance to another, there were often *radical* differences. The most astonishing thing was that when confronted with that evidence, the bards themselves said "Well, it *is* accurate."

Others have concluded from this that in a culture that is primarily oral, accuracy is not equated with verbatim agreement.

Verbatim agreement might not even exist as a concept. Without the technology to preserve the word, such as writing or a recording device, it simply does not occur to people that verbatim accuracy would be desirable. In such a culture, accuracy means something like rendering the tradition in a way that is faithful. That's what you have in earliest Christianity—people passing on sayings, stories and the like, attempting to be faithful to the tradition but not aiming for verbatim accuracy.

That is why verbatim agreement between Matthew and Luke is so striking. When two authors rely on oral tradition, such extensive verbatim agreement is very unlikely. It happens only when two authors happen to be using a third author's work as their common starting point. In this case, that work was Q.

Where are the oldest physical texts of Matthew, Mark and Luke found? If scholars want to study the actual written word, where should they go?

The oldest biblical manuscript for one of the Gospels is Papyrus 52, a fragment that belongs to the John Rylands Library in Manchester, England. It dates to around 125 C.E. Unfortunately, it is no bigger than the palm of my hand and contains only a small fragment of John, chapter 18. Of roughly equal age is Papyrus Egerton, which contains fragments of an unknown, noncanonical gospel referred to as the Egerton Gospel. Unfortunately, all of the earliest biblical manuscripts are quite fragmentary like this. Even the earliest manuscripts are several decades, even a century or more removed from the original writing of the texts they contain. The earliest complete Gospel texts we have date to the fourth century, roughly three hundred years after the originals were written. Scholars must rely on these relatively late copies of earlier copies of earlier copies, etc., to reconstruct the original text of the Gospels. One of these complete Gospel texts is located here in Washington at the Freer Museum. It is called Codex W, and it dates to the fifth century.

Reconstructing the Gospel texts is very technical, time consuming work. It involves the analysis of literally hundreds of texts and fragments. Naturally these manuscripts, some of them extremely valuable, are scattered throughout the world in various libraries and museums. To study them all, one might go to the Ancient Biblical Manuscript Center at Claremont University, which keeps a fairly complete collection of manuscripts on microfilm. But it takes a brave soul to enter that field of study.

II. THE PALESTINIAN BACKGROUND FOR A LIFE OF JESUS

I want to begin with a couple of brief thank-yous and a word of introduction before I turn to my topic, the Palestinian background for a life of Jesus. I thank Hershel Shanks for pulling this event together and for inviting me to be part of this. It is, quite frankly, an honor for a small-town boy from North Dakota to be here. I also want to thank all of you for being here this morning.

I love doing this. My wife tells me I'm always at my best in front of a large group of people—which has always seemed somewhat of a double-edged remark. But, so it goes...

I live in two different professional worlds. On the one hand, I live in the world of the secular academy. My teaching position is at a state university supported by public funds, and the professional organizations in which I am most active are all committed to the nonsectarian study of Jesus and Christian origins. In those settings, it is inappropriate to approach the study of Jesus with specifically Christian presuppositions or with his significance for Christian faith in mind.

I also live in the world of the church. I grew up in the church, and I am actively involved in church life and worship. My wife is an Episcopal priest, so I am even married to a priest, which, I must admit, was not one of my childhood fantasies. I mention the fact that I live in two different worlds so that you will know that it's possible to combine the two—the academic study of Jesus and being a Christian. What I will be presenting to you today will flow from the first of those worlds, although I would be happy to respond to questions that also have to do with the second.

As you have already heard from Hershel Shanks and Steve Patterson, this is an exciting time in historical Jesus research. There is a renaissance going on, and it's a very rich time to be a Jesus scholar. Part of that renaissance is a much greater knowledge of the social world of first-century Jewish Palestine, my topic in this lecture—the Palestinian background for a life of Jesus, or as I would subtitle it, the social world of Jesus. The main portion of my talk will concern what we know about that social world, but I want to begin with a brief prologue in which I will speak about two things—how and why we know more and the highly useful notion of social world.

How and why do we know so much more about the social world of Jesus than we did 50 years ago? There are primarily two reasons. We have new data, and we have new lenses. Our new data comes primarily from two sources. Some of it comes from ongoing archaeological research, which I won't say anything more about at this point, except that it continues to increase enormously our knowledge of that world. Some of our new data comes from manuscript discoveries during the past 50 years, the most important of which for a Palestinian environment are the Dead Sea Scrolls. And your host today, Hershel Shanks, as I think most of you know, has been instrumental in bringing about the publication of the remainder of these. He's been courageous, even heroic, in doing that, and we are grateful to him.

Minimally, these scrolls tell us firsthand about the beliefs and practices of a Jewish sectarian movement, the Essenes. Maximally, these scrolls may be a library containing documents from a number of different Jewish groups, though I am skeptical about this myself. But the point is that we have an enormous amount of new data.

Now, in addition to all of this new data, we also have new lenses for seeing or viewing that data. These lenses come from the emerging interdisciplinary character of historical Jesus research. We increasingly make use of insights and models drawn from cultural anthropology, sociology, psychology, the history of religion and so forth. Using these disciplines, we have produced models and insights that greatly illuminate our texts by illuminating that world. Models of religious protest movements, of pre-industrial agrarian societies, of purity societies, of honor-shame societies and more enable us to see the data in new ways. They enable us to constellate the data into meaningful patterns, a *Gestalt*, that we otherwise would not see. So we have new data, and we have new lenses; that's the how and the why of our new knowledge.

My second prologue remark is to provide you with a definition of the highly useful notion of social world. I begin by quoting the opening of British novelist L. P. Hartley's novel *The Go-Between.*[1] It is a great line: "The past is a foreign country. They do things differently there." The point of the quote is that there is an enormous distance between us and the world of the past. The distance between us and that world is not just temporal (not simply that it was a long time ago) or conceptual (they thought differently). It is also social, and the social distance means differences in social structures, social roles, social values and general cultural features. As Bruce Malina and Richard Rohrbaugh, in their recent book *Social Science Commentary on the Synoptic Gospels,*[2] suggest, the social distance may be the most fundamental distance of all between us and the world of the distant past.

A useful way to highlight that social distance is with the notion of "social world." Social world means the total social environment in which people live. That social environment has both material and nonmaterial elements. The material elements, which are basically the visible elements, include such things as population density, degree of urbanization, level of technology, distribution of wealth and so forth. The nonmaterial elements may be even more important. The nonmaterial elements of social world include a society's shared understandings, meanings, values and laws and the institutions that embody them. Social world is basically a culture's social construction of reality. Or to put it slightly differently, social world is what makes a particular culture what it is.

I sometimes try to explain this to my students by telling them that social world is what makes Oregon Oregon and not, for example, Pakistan. Certainly there are geographical, climatic and topographical differences between Oregon and Pakistan, but the really huge differences between Oregon and Pakistan are social, the very different social constructions of reality operative in each place.

That's what I want to talk about this morning, the social world of first-century Jewish Palestine, the canopy of shared meanings and understandings within which that culture lived.

I note at the outset what a small-scale social world we are talking about, how compact the social world of first-century Jewish Palestine was. First-century Jewish Palestine was approximately 150 miles long from north to south, with an average width of 50 miles. That's 7,500 square miles, which is one-thirteenth the size of the state of Oregon, or to choose an example closer at hand, five-sixths the size of the state of Maryland. The Sea of Galilee, in fact, is really a freshwater lake approximately twelve miles by seven miles. The Jordan River, one of the most famous rivers in the world, is only 100 miles long.

Population centers were also small. Jerusalem, the major city, had about 40,000 people. Sepphoris, the largest city in Galilee, also had about 40,000 people. And the village of Nazareth has been variously estimated from about 200 people to 1,500 people. The point is we are talking about a small-scale social world.

As I describe that social world, I will emphasize two things. The first is that it was a deeply Jewish social world, and the second is that the central cultural characteristics were also deeply Jewish.

It's important to emphasize the deeply Jewish character for at least two reasons. One, it enables us to see that world. If we don't see the Jewishness, we don't see that social world. And two, it's important because it is easy to forget the Jewish character of Jesus and the early Jesus movement and, for that matter, early Christianity throughout much of the first century. Not only were Jesus and the disciples Jewish, but the authors of all the New Testament books, with the possible exception of Luke-Acts, were also Jewish. In the church in particular, this sometimes slips from our awareness, and we think of Jesus primarily as the founder of Christianity.

Elisabeth Schüssler Fiorenza of Harvard Divinity School tells a great story about one of her colleagues doing an adult education class in a local church. The church happened to be Catholic, which matters for the end of the story. Schüssler Fiorenza says this colleague of hers worked very hard to convince her audience that Jesus was really Jewish and that his disciples were Jewish. The audience finally accepted that, and then a voice came from the back of the room, "But surely his mother wasn't Jewish."[3]

When I say Jesus' world was a deeply Jewish social world, one of the things I mean is that it was grounded in the Scriptures of ancient Israel, basically the Law and the Prophets at the time of Jesus, so that the canopy under which that social world lived was a sacred canopy.

That world had two primary pillars, two centers, to change the image slightly. The two pillars were Torah and Temple. The Torah—by which I mean the Pentateuch, the five books of Moses, the first five books of the Hebrew Bible—was the foundation of Israel's world view and ethos, the foundation of its image of reality and its way of life. The Pentateuch contained the stories that shaped their way of seeing as well as their sense of identity. It was what the Old Testament scholar Walter Brueggemann calls "Israel's primal narrative, the most important narrative they knew and the narrative they believed was decisively true about them."[4] The Torah contained their stories of creation, of God entering into a covenant with Abraham and the promises attached to it, of the liberation from slavery in Egypt, of the giving of the law at Mount Sinai, the wandering in the wilderness and the gift of the land.

In addition to that identity-shaping story, the Torah was also the source of the laws and, in a sense, of the whole legal system of first-century Jewish Palestine. It contained not just what we would think of as religious or moral laws, but also criminal laws, civil laws, domestic laws. It was the law of the culture. There was no religious law separate from secular law. The Torah was the source of all laws. Thus both world view and ethos were grounded in the first pillar of the Jewish social world.

The second pillar, or center, was the Temple in Jerusalem. The importance of the Temple can be described this way. Rather than saying the Temple was in Jerusalem, we should say Jerusalem was a small city built around the Temple. The Temple was the symbolic and cosmological center of the Jewish universe. It was God's dwelling place on earth, the point of contact between this world and the other world, the world of spirit. As such, the Temple was the navel of the earth, the umbilical cord connecting this world to the world that gave birth to it. As the place of God's presence, the Temple was the center of both worship and devotion. Only there could sacrifices be offered, and it was the destination of pilgrimages.

The Temple was not only the religious center, but also the economic and political center of the Jewish social world.

It was the central bank in Jewish Palestine, and to it flowed the tithes commanded by the Torah, for tithing was basically taxation. The Temple was also the center of the native Jewish aristocracy, the high priestly families who ruled in collaboration with Rome.

This social world was maintained or sustained by various practices. There were three major annual festivals, the festival of Passover, which remembered the Exodus, the festival of Pentecost, which remembered the giving of the law on Mount Sinai, and the festival of Tabernacles, which recalled the years of wandering in the wilderness.

In addition to these annual festivals, there was the Sabbath, a weekly remembrance and celebration of the reality of God. And, of course, there was Torah observance, which covered all aspects of life. All of these sustained the social world.

It is important to recognize that there was also diversity within Judaism, so that scholars appropriately speak of a variety of Judaisms in the first century. Nevertheless, amongst all those varieties of Judaisms, there was unanimity about the importance of the two institutions, Torah and Temple. Indeed, the differences among various Jewish groups might best be seen as differences about how to understand Torah and Temple.

Now I move to my second main point, the central cultural dynamics of Jesus' social world. I will identify five cultural dynamics that enable us to see what was going on in that world. After I have identified each one, I will in most cases provide an illustration or two from the Gospels to suggest why an awareness of this cultural dynamic is illuminating in order to suggest something about its explanatory power. I have condensed this—not the whole thing but the subheads—into five words. Three of them start with P, and I worked very hard to make the other two start with P, for alliterative purposes, but finally gave up. I could do so only by putting the emphasis on the second or third syllable, which gets weird. So there are two C's and three P's as central cultural dynamics of Jesus' social world: colonial, cosmopolitan, peasant, purity and patriarchal.

To begin with the first one, Jesus lived in a colonial society. The P word here was im-Perial. (We'll let that go!) Jewish Palestine was a colony of the Roman Empire and had been since 63 B.C.E. Palestine was important to Roman imperial policy for at least two reasons. It was the land bridge to Egypt, the breadbasket of the empire; and it was a buffer against the Parthian empire to the east, Rome's only serious rival in that part of the world. Rome ruled Palestine sometimes through client kings, such as the Herods, and sometimes directly through Roman governors in cooperation with the native Jewish aristocracy.

Economically, Roman rule brought another layer of taxation to Palestine. Religiously and politically, Roman rule conflicted with the Jewish vision of Israel as a free people living in their own land. Roman rule also brought a stronger gentile presence and a proliferation of gentile practices. Roman governors were often insensitive to Jewish religious beliefs and practices and were sometimes brutal.

Thus the two centuries from 63 B.C.E. to the time of the Second Jewish Revolt (132 to 135 C.E.) were marked by unrest and turmoil. There were spontaneous popular demonstrations, nonviolent social protests, social banditry, popular prophetic movements, armed uprisings and wars. The most catastrophic of these upheavals was the Great Jewish Revolt from 66 to 70, which climaxed in the destruction of Jerusalem and the Temple, probably the most disastrous event experienced by the Jewish people in their ancient history, paralleled only by the Babylonian destruction of Jerusalem and the Temple some 600 years earlier.

This whole period of time (from the beginning of Roman rule to the suppression of the Second Jewish Revolt) was marked by what Richard Horsley has called "the spiral of violence,"[5] a spiral that begins with the violence of systemic injustice (the violence built into the system itself) and moves to protest against that injustice, then to repressive countermeasures to put down the protests and finally to open revolt against the establishment. Jesus lived in a colonial society and in a generation headed toward war.

Second, Jesus lived in a cosmopolitan society, a society that was in contact with other cultures, especially Hellenism, and was affected by them. Cultural contact with Hellenism began in the fourth century B.C.E., at the time of Alexander the Great's conquests. To some extent, all of Judaism had been Hellenized by the first century with, of course, important differences of degree.

This means that Galilee was more pluralistic and perhaps more urbanized than most of us have commonly imagined. Let me give you a few examples of this from Galilee. First is the use of Greek. Recent archaeological finds suggest that the use of Greek was much more widespread than we thought, and this creates the very real possibility that Jesus, and perhaps the disciples, were bilingual. And maybe not just touristically bilingual but functionally bilingual. If that's the case, though we still whisper about this in scholarly circles, it's even conceivable that Jesus may sometimes have taught in Greek and not just in Aramaic.

There was international trade. We know that beer was imported into Galilee from both Egypt and Babylon. The city of Sepphoris, which I mentioned briefly earlier, was the largest city in Galilee and was located only four miles from Nazareth. Sepphoris was destroyed by the Romans in 4 B.C.E. when a rebellion at the time of the death of Herod the Great was put down. The city was rebuilt during the childhood and young adulthood of Jesus.

If the tradition that Jesus was a *tekton*, a worker in wood, is correct, it is possible that Jesus may even have been involved in the reconstruction of Sepphoris. We don't know that, but it's an interesting speculation. Sepphoris was cosmopolitan. With its large population, it probably attracted healers and, perhaps, some cynic sages. It's hard to know what Jesus may have seen when he went to Sepphoris. It's reasonable to suppose that a bright Jewish boy like Jesus would have gone there a number of times.

A theater has even been discovered in Sepphoris, a Greco-Roman style theater, seating about 3,000 people. There is some uncertainty about whether this theater was built during the lifetime of Jesus or later. But if it was there during his lifetime, he may very well have gone to the theater. If he did go to the theater, he would have seen actors wearing masks, as they did in Greco-Roman theaters everywhere. The word for an actor performing behind a mask is *hypocrite*. Thus the word *hypocrite* could come from Jesus' experience of the theater. In short, our image of Galilee as a rural backwater isolated from the rest of the world has changed.

A third characteristic of the social world of Jesus is that it was a peasant society. By this I do not simply mean that there were a lot of peasants, although there were. Rather, peasant society is a shorthand phrase for a particular type of society, namely "pre-industrial agrarian society" as described by Gerhard Lenski.[6] These societies are known widely throughout the premodern world.

The defining characteristic of a pre-industrial agrarian society is that it's a two-class society. On the one hand, there are urban ruling elites, and on the other hand, there are rural peasants. The rural peasants typically comprise approximately 90 percent of the population. To flesh out that grand contrast just a bit, the urban ruling elites consist of five groups: the ruler; the governing class; the retainers (retainers are basically employees of the ruler and the governing class); the well-to-do merchants; and the upper echelon of the priesthood. The ruler and governing class are about one percent of the population and typically receive about half of the income. The elites together (ten percent of the population) typically receive two-thirds of the income. The rural peasants include small land-holders as well as sharecroppers, day laborers, unclean and degraded classes and expendables.

There's a huge gulf between these two classes. Peasant societies are marked by sharp social and economic inequalities. There is no middle class. To try to illustrate that with two contrasting diagrams, all of us are familiar with the pyramid diagram of modern societies—a fairly small upper class, a larger middle class and an even larger lower class. A peasant society would not be diagrammed as a pyramid. The best analogy I can think of is one of those old-fashioned oilcans with a broad bottom and a long narrow spout coming up out of it. The vast majority of people are represented by that broad bottom and the urban ruling elites by the needlelike spout rising vertically from the base.

Where do the urban ruling elites (not just in first-century Jewish Palestine but generally in societies like this) get their wealth? They don't manufacture anything. They don't produce anything. They don't grow anything. I'm not even sure they provide any services. They get their wealth, of course, from the peasants, and they get it in two forms—rent for land and taxation. Peasant societies are thus economically oppressive and exploitative.

This awareness illuminates the Gospels and what the Gospels say about Jesus in a number of ways. I'll mention just a couple for illustrative purposes. When Jesus speaks about his message being "good news to the poor" or when he says "blessed are the poor," it's pretty clear, I think, that he's talking about real poor people. This is not a metaphor. He is talking about the oppressed group in a peasant society.

The teaching of Jesus also includes a number of indictments. The indictments are not of society as a whole but of the elites. Jesus' primary social conflict was with the elites. This is illuminating when we think about the causes of the death of Jesus. In all likelihood, a combination of Roman authority and a narrow circle of the Jewish ruling elites was responsible for his arrest and execution. Very importantly, rather than Jesus being rejected, arrested and executed by "the Jews" or the Jewish people, the final and fatal conflict was with urban ruling elites who, rather than representing the Jewish people, were in fact oppressors of most Jewish people.

The fourth characteristic of Jesus' social world was purity. Purity societies are known in many cultures, both before and since the time of Jesus. Indeed, there are still residues of purity societies in our own time. A purity society is organized around the great contrast or polarity between pure and impure. Purity and impurity apply to persons, groups, places, things and times.

Most important for our purposes is the way that purity and impurity got attached to people and social groups. The pure, of course, were people who observed the purity laws. The impure were the nonobservant, and the worst of the nonobservant were outcasts or untouchables. The notion of an untouchable is only apropos in a purity system.

This contrast also got attached to other basic contrasts in the society. It got attached to the contrast between righteous people and sinners. The righteous were observant; sinners, generally speaking, were nonobservant. It's very interesting what happens to the notion of sin in a purity system. Sinners become untouchables. It became attached to the contrast between whole and not whole, in a physical sense. If you were chronically ill or maimed or had crushed testicles or something terrible like that, you were permanently impure. Wholeness, again, went with purity. It also got attached to the contrast between rich and poor. To be rich didn't automatically make you pure, but to be poor tended to put you on the impure side of the spectrum. It got attached to the contrast between male and female and the contrast between Jew and gentile.

All of this created a social world with sharp social boundaries. The usefulness of the concept of a purity society for understanding Jesus and early Christianity is pervasive, it seems to me. One of the central characteristics of Jesus' public activity was open-table fellowship, or what Dom Crossan calls "open commensality,"[7] eating meals with people of all sorts. A purity system creates closed-table fellowship, or "closed commensality." What was at stake in Jesus' open-table practice—and it's useful to remember that this is the ancestor of the Christian Eucharist or mass or Lord's Supper—was an alternative social vision that radically challenged the purity system.

The Gospels also report a number of purity disputes about the washing of hands and utensils and things like that. It's easy for us, from a modern point of view, to see these as trivial. But they weren't trivial; in that world, purity was political. It was embedded in the social system; it structured the society; and thus Jesus' table practices and the disputes about purity concerned the shape of his world.

The fifth and final central characteristic of Jesus' social world is that it was a patriarchal society. In this it was like most premodern cultures and, to some extent, contemporary cultures as well. The more complete formula is that it was an androcentric and patriarchal society. The word androcentric refers to a way of seeing, to a perspective, namely seeing the world through male eyes. In this sense much of the biblical tradition is androcentric.

A quick illustration. Most of you are familiar with the Book of Proverbs and that there are a number of sayings about wives in it. There are sayings about difficult wives, fretful wives and a marvelous chapter about ideal wives. There are no sayings in the Book of Proverbs about difficult husbands, fretful husbands or, for that matter, about ideal husbands. Well, why not? Because the book was written by men and for men. It's androcentric.

Patriarchy, on the other hand, refers to a social system, and it refers specifically to a hierarchical social system in which some men rule over other men and over all women and children. Patriarchy refers both to the structure of the society as a whole and to the structure of the family. The patriarchal family structure was a microcosm of the social structure.

The system of patriarchy is not peculiar to Judaism. All the cultures surrounding Judaism were patriarchal as well. Patriarchy was typical in that part of the world, in all parts of the world, in fact.

This system radically affected how women were seen and what roles they played in society. Women were profoundly second-class citizens. They were separated from men in public life. They were veiled when they went out. They were not to be taught the Torah, incidentally. Let me explain that briefly. Everybody learned basic Torah practices just from growing up in the culture. It was part of socialization, just as we learn most of our cultural customs just from growing up. But women were not to be taught the Torah in the sense of being taught how to interpret the texts. Why not? Lots of reasons were given, but perhaps the most compelling one is that the ability to interpret Torah was a form of power, and if you let women start playing with those texts, there's no telling what they might come up with.

Again, I want to stress that this was not peculiar to Judaism. The usefulness of keeping this in mind is probably already apparent to you. All of the stories about Jesus and women in the Gospels constitute a radical challenge to patriarchy. But it goes beyond that. All of you are familiar with the anti-family sayings in the Gospels. (The Gospels are not in favor of family values.) The anti-family sayings in the Gospels need to be understood in the context of the patriarchal family. They are invitations to leave the patriarchal family as the center of security and identity.

One other quick illustration, from chapter 23 of Matthew, a short verse that Jesus may or may not have said: "Call no man on earth your father, for you have but one Father who is in heaven." The analogy goes like this. Call no one on earth your lord, for you have but one Lord who is God. That is, just as the lordship of God rules out all earthly lords, so in this case, the fatherhood of God rules out all earthly fathers. It's a fascinating instance of the fatherhood of God being used in a subversive and anti-patriarchal way.

That completes the list of central cultural dynamics operating in the social world of Jesus. There is more that could be said. For example, it was also a patronal society, in which patron-client relationships were central, an honor-shame society, in which the preservation of honor and the avoidance of shame were central concerns. But I hope I have shown how a better understanding of the social world of Jesus is useful (I would say indispensable) for understanding the traditions about Jesus.

As I move to my conclusion, I want to stress that we should not think of what I have just described as if it were Judaism itself, as if it were *the* Judaism of the first century. For there were many different Jewish voices in this society—reform and renewal movements, popular prophetic movements, individual Jewish saints, mystics and purveyors of peasant wisdom. Jesus and the Jesus movement were among those alternative voices.

What I have described was the climate, the social world, in which these various Jewish voices struggled, and to some extent competed, with each other. Their intention was to articulate and embody a vision of faithfulness to God and the traditions of Israel in that turbulent century. Eventually, out of that social world and the events of that century flowed the two streams of Judaism—rabbinic Judaism and early Christianity, both destined to become world religions persisting to this day. But that time had not yet come, and thus we see Jesus and the early Jesus movement most clearly when we see them as Jewish voices in the world of first-century Jewish Palestine.

ENDNOTES

1. Leslie P. Hartley, *The Go-Between* (New York: Stein and Day, 1953).

2. Bruce J. Malina and Richard Rohrbaugh, *Social Science Commentary on the Synoptic Gospels* (Minneapolis: Fortress, 1992).

3. Elisabeth Schüssler Fiorenza, *In Memory of Her: A Feminist Theological Reconstruction of Christian Origins* (New York: Crossroad, 1983), pp. 105-106.

4. Walter Brueggemann, *The Bible Makes Sense* (Atlanta: John Knox, 1977), pp. 45-46.

5. Richard Horsley, *Jesus and the Spiral of Violence* (San Francisco: Harper & Row, 1987).

6. Gerhard Lenski, *Power and Privilege: A Theory of Social Stratification* (New York: McGraw-Hill, 1966).

7. John Dominic Crossan, *The Historical Jesus: The Life of a Mediterranean Jewish Peasant* (HarperSanFrancisco, 1992), esp. pp. 341-344; *Jesus: A Revolutionary Biography* (HarperSanFrancisco, 1994), pp. 66-74.

QUESTIONS & ANSWERS

Has Geza Vermes' understanding of Jesus the Jew held up?

What is central to Vermes' understanding of Jesus the Jew is that Jesus was a charismatic Galilean holy man. That means a man of deeds, a healer. Vermes claims there were a number of these people in first-century Jewish Palestine. He also complicates that a little bit by seeing them as prototypes of the Hasidim. My understanding of the scholarly discussion following the publication of Vermes' book of 20 years ago, *Jesus the Jew* (Collins, 1973; Fortress, 1981), is that there is agreement that there were Galilean charismatics, but the connection Vermes makes between them and the Hasidim is probably weak.

Has Vermes' assertion that Jesus was part of the small middle class held up?

In that culture, artisans, like carpenters, were not above the landholding small peasant class but actually below. To be an artisan or a carpenter was to be from a family that had lost its land. That suggests that to be a carpenter is to be on the marginalized edge of the peasant class.

In terms of social class, what do you make of the Gospel writers' emphasis on the education of Jesus? Several times, some of his opponents say he is a carpenter's son. Or of Luke's account of the young boy debating with the doctors of the law? Was this understood by the early Christian community as Jesus having a kind of supernatural knowledge of Torah,

or would his knowledge have been the same as any adult Jew would have acquired, even an illiterate Jew?

The story of Jesus debating the law with the experts in the Temple at age 12 is almost certainly legendary. So we can let go of that right away as part of the evidential base.

Second, the comments about the adult Jesus in the Gospel have to do with his brightness and quickness, and they don't necessarily imply that he had a scribal awareness of the Torah or other sacred texts. Here I'll point out a possible area of disagreement, a minor one, between Dom Crossan and me. As I understand Dom, he doesn't think Jesus had a scribal awareness. I'm not so sure of that myself. But we don't need to go into that right now; I'll just note there is some difference there.

The other thing that I can say is that, as the tradition develops into the second and third centuries, in the post-canonical gospels, stories emerge of the very young Jesus having a supernatural kind of knowledge that he could not possibly have learned. So there was a tendency in the early community in the post-Easter decades to begin to ascribe to Jesus qualities that went beyond human qualities. For example, there's this irritating story in the infancy gospel of Thomas about Jesus bamboozling the teachers of the law, I think, at age six. You would just want to hit this kid because he goes on and on uttering these nonsense questions, and this is supposed to show he's really bright. But the point is that he was increasingly said to have had this kind of supernatural ability.

In response to your lighthearted humor, was Mary Jewish?

Well, I'll simply say yes. I don't know that I have any better response than that.

III. THE INFANCY AND YOUTH OF THE MESSIAH

The question is often raised about the "lost years of Jesus." Why are we given the infancy story and then nothing until he's an adult? The question really is based on a misunderstanding of the infancy narratives. They are not the first chapter, chapter one of the life of Jesus, with, as it were, chapters two and three (Jesus grows up, Jesus goes to college) missing, and then the adult life of Jesus. The infancy narratives are overtures, not first acts but overtures. The function of an overture is to give you a musical medley, a thematic overview of what is to come. Usually overtures are written after the play has been completed. The infancy stories, therefore, must be taken as overtures, not first acts or first chapters.

Each Gospel has an overture. Two of them (Matthew and Luke) have infancy stories as overtures. There are no lost sections in those two Gospels. The first section is an overture, and then you go straight into the story.

When you read those two stories in Matthew 1-2 and Luke 1-2, the first thing that should strike you is that they are totally different. Even if we can get them organized and get the Magi and the shepherds around the crib so we don't notice the problem, they're totally different. But of course they *should* be totally different if they are overtures to different Gospels.

The Surface Level: Luke 1-2 and Matthew 1-2. The first layer explains what Luke is doing and what Matthew is doing. Basically, Luke is comparing Jesus and John the Baptist in order to exalt Jesus over John the Baptist. But not just over John the Baptist. Just as Jesus is born of a virgin, or at least conceived virginally, so John the Baptist is born of aged, infertile parents. And that immediately subsumes the birth of Isaac, the great patriarch, and the birth of Samuel, the great prophet, also born of aged and/or infertile parents. So Luke 1-2 is an exaltation of Jesus over the patriarchal and prophetic traditions of Israel.

To do this, Luke tells his story in five acts. Imagine the story as a drama. The first act is the *Angelic Annunciations* (Luke 1:5-25 and 1:26-38). There is one annunciation to Zachary about John's conception and another annunciation to Mary about Jesus' conception. Each angel says, "Do not be afraid." Each recipient asks a question. Zachary says, "How will I know this is so? I am an old man, my wife is getting on in years." Mary says, "How can this be since I am a virgin?" The first act is parallel *Angelic Annunciations.*

The second act is the *Publicized Birth* of each child (Luke 1:57-58 and 2:7-14). That of John: "Her neighbors and relatives heard that the Lord had shown his great mercy to her, and they rejoiced with her." And then, of course, you get to the birth of Jesus in much more detail—the manger in the stable because the inn had no place for them and the shepherds in the fields terrified then reassured by the angelic hosts of heaven.

The third act is *Circumcision and Naming* (Luke 1:59-63a and 2:21). So far, then, we've had Angelic Annunciations, Publicized Births and the Circumcision and Naming of each child. I'm not reading the full texts to you, but you can do that with your own Bible. What you notice is parallelism, but the score keeps coming up John: 0, Jesus: 1. In the circumcision and naming of John, "on the eighth day, they came to circumcise the child, and they were going to name him Zachary but were told he was to be called John." Jesus, "after eight days had passed and it was time to circumcise the child, he was called Jesus, the name given by the angel before he was conceived in the womb."

The fourth act is the *Public Presentation and Prophesy of Destiny* for each child (Luke 1:65-79 and 2:21-38). Again, parallelism, but also the subtle or not-so-subtle exaltation of Jesus. John is born and "fear came over all their neighbors and these things were talked about throughout the entire hill country of Judea....Zachary was filled with the Holy Spirit" and speaks in prophecy about John but mostly about Jesus. Unlike John, the public presentation of Jesus is in the Temple, not a house in the Judean hills, but in the Temple. And again, there is prophecy, this time two prophecies, Simon *and* Anna, male *and* female. Furthermore, both prophecies focus mostly on Jesus, whereas the prophecy about the destiny of John is mostly about Jesus. John is destined to speak of Jesus.

The fifth act is *Description of the Child's Growth* (Luke 1:80 and 2:40-52). Once again, John comes first, and, once again, Jesus wins. For example, first, "The child [John] grew and became strong in spirit, and he was in the wilderness until the day he appeared publicly to Israel." Then, "The child [Jesus] grew and became strong, filled with *wisdom*, and the *favor of God* was upon him." But then, of course, comes the climax. The story about Jesus' parents finding him in the Temple when he was 12, "sitting among the teachers, listening to them and asking them questions; and all who heard him were amazed at his understanding and his answers....and Jesus increased in *wisdom* and stature and *favor with God* and man." Notice how the italicized phrases frame that scene, and the entire complex of 2:40-52. Jesus overpowers completely the single phrase in 1:80 for John.

Basically that is what Luke does. He constructs a five-act drama in which Jesus is parallel but superior to John the Baptist. John the Baptist is born, as was, for example, Isaac and Samuel, of aged and/or infertile parents. Jesus is born of a virginal conception. Jesus is overwhelmingly superior to the prophetic and the patriarchal traditions of his people.

Now turn to Matthew. In a way, Matthew accomplishes the same thing but in a totally different way. Matthew compares the infancy of Jesus with the infancy of Moses. But to complicate the matter, the infancy of Moses is not the same as in Exodus 1-2. At the time of Jesus, popular traditions expanded that rather terse account of the infancy of Moses, and those popular versions are important for the Matthew parallelism. I will be talking here not just about the bare bones of the story in Exodus, but also about popular expansions in, say, the

Targumim, or Aramaic paraphrase translations of the Bible, and the Midrashim, or commentaries expanding on the biblical text. We know that a long tradition of popular expansion was already present in the first century because we find it in summary both in Josephus' *Antiquities of the Jews* (4.254-59) and in a book called *Liber Antiquitatum Biblicarum* (9.2-10), which was first wrongly attributed to Philo, so now it's called pseudo-Philo.[1]

Why were there popular expansions? Anyone who reads about the birth of Moses in Exodus 1-2 can tell you it's not a very good story. First of all, Pharaoh sets out to kill all the Israelites. And just by bad luck, as it were, Moses happens to be born at that time. That is a sort of transcendental tackiness. Was it just coincidence? Surely, somehow, Moses was at the center. Surely the children were being killed in order to get Moses. And that's exactly how the popular traditions make it happen.

Second, why would the Israelites go on having children if their male infants were going to be killed? Why didn't they simply stop having children? Again, the popular expansions, pinpointing where they see problems in the text, address those questions.

Let me talk again about a drama, this time a drama with three acts divided into scenes. We're looking at Matthew's account of the infancy of Jesus in parallel with and exaltation over the infancy of Moses. But notice, of course, that if patriarchs, prophets, Moses and the law aren't important, you don't bother doing this. This is all a debate within Judaism.

The first act of Moses' and Jesus' births is the *Ruler's Plot*. This act has four scenes. I call them *Sign, Fear, Consultation* and *Massacre*. Notice how exactly parallel they are in both accounts.

Here's what happens in the popular accounts. Pharaoh dreamed he was sitting on his throne and saw an old man before him with a merchant's balance in his hand. The old man took all the elders, princes and nobles of Egypt and put them on one scale of the balance. Then he took a lamb and put it on the second scale, and the lamb outweighed them all. Pharaoh wondered about this terrible vision, but then he awoke to find it was only a dream. That *Sign* is the first scene of the *Ruler's Plot*.

The second scene is *Fear*. The next morning, Pharaoh arose, summoned all his courtiers, narrated his dream, and everyone was extremely frightened.

Consultation is the third scene. The courtiers explain that a great evil must be coming upon Egypt. What is it? A child will be born in Israel who will destroy the land of Egypt. They accordingly ask that a royal statute be written and promulgated throughout the land of Egypt to kill every newborn male of the Hebrews so that this evil will be averted.

Now, at last, we have the story properly told. The point of the *Massacre* is to kill Moses, who is soon to be born. The story in Exodus continues about the massacre of all newborn males *in order* to kill Moses.

When you look through that lens at Matthew, you see something very similar. There is a *Sign* (Matthew 2:1-2). In the time of King Herod, wise men come from the East asking, "Where is the child?" There is *Fear* (Matthew 2:3). "When King Herod heard this, he was frightened, and all Jerusalem with him," just like Pharaoh and his court. There is *Consultation* (Matthew 2:4-6). "Calling together all the chief priests and scribes of the people, he inquired of them where the Messiah was to be born. They told him 'In Bethlehem.'" So Herod decrees the *Massacre* (Matthew 2:7-8,16-18). *Sign, Fear, Consultation, Massacre.* Exact parallelism.

The first act, with four scenes, is the *Ruler's Plot.* We now have a parallel. Pharaoh kills the children in order to kill Moses. Herod kills the children in order to kill Jesus.

The second act is the *Father's Decision.* All you have in Exodus is that, "A man from the house of Levi went and married a Levite woman. The woman conceived and bore a son" (Exodus 2:1). But, as I asked before, why did they do that if they knew the child might be killed? That question is answered in the popular accounts.

The *Father's Decision* has three scenes: *Divorce, Reassurance, Remarriage.* The *Divorce* scene narrates how some Israelites, when they heard the decree ordained by Pharaoh that their male children would be killed, divorced their wives, but the rest stayed married. The second scene is *Reassurance.* The spirit of God comes on Miriam, Moses-to-be's elder sister, and she announces that a son will be born to her father and mother who will save Israel from the power of Egypt. The final scene is *Remarriage.* Amram listens to Miriam and remarries his wife.

When you look at Matthew through that lens, you see those same three scenes for the birth of Jesus. There is the *Divorce* scene in Matthew 1:18-19 where Joseph, piously but lethally, "being a righteous man and unwilling to expose her to public disgrace, planned to dismiss her quietly." The *Reassurance* episode follows in Matthew 1:20-23 where "an angel of the Lord appeared to him in a dream and said 'Joseph, son of David, do not be afraid to take Mary as your wife, for the child conceived in her is from the Holy Spirit.'" Finally, there is the *Remarriage* scene in Matthew 1:24: "When Joseph awoke from sleep, he did as the angel of the Lord commanded him; he took her as his wife, but had no marital relations with her until she had borne a son; and he named him Jesus."

The third and final act of the drama is the *Child's Deliverance.* The popular accounts of Moses' birth make no attempt to improve on the Exodus story of Nile bulrushes and Pharaoh's daughter. Matthew's account makes little attempt to continue the detailed parallelism into the third and final act. But in that last act, parallelism turns ironic. Jesus flees and takes refuge in, of all places, Egypt.

That's the first level: Matthew compares Jesus with Moses, and thence with the legal traditions; Luke compares Jesus with John the Baptist, and thence with the patriarchal and prophetic traditions. Both use parallelism to exalt Jesus. Both do exactly the same thing in totally different ways. But isn't this a little too coincidental—to do exactly the same thing, even if in different ways?

The Middle Level: Virginal Conception and Bethlehem Birth. Now let's move down to the second, deeper level—the virginal conception and Bethlehem birth of Jesus. These are two things on which Matthew and Luke agree. They disagree on almost everything else except maybe the names of Jesus, Mary and Joseph and a few minor details. And that a child was born. It's sort of useful in an infancy story for somebody to be born.

Born of the Virgin Mary. Matthew, notice this, makes an explicit reference to Isaiah 7:14 in 1:20-23. "'Joseph, son of David, do not be afraid to take Mary as your wife, for the child conceived in her is from the Holy Spirit. She will bear a son, and you are to name him Jesus, for he will save his people from their sins.' All this took place to fulfill what had been spoken by the Lord through the prophet: 'Look the virgin shall conceive and bear a son, and they shall call him Emmanuel,' which means God with us.' " The prophet cited is Isaiah 7:14, who spoke in Hebrew about an *'almâ*, a virgin married but not yet pregnant with her first child. In Greek the word was translated as *parthenos*, which in this context meant the same thing, a newly married woman, presumably a virgin, who will have her first child soon. Matthew reads this prophecy of Isaiah as one of hope. She will conceive and remain a virgin. He takes it literally and applies it to the virginal conception of Jesus.

Let me stop here for a second. I've used the word prophecy. Imagine two different kinds of prophecy. I call them projective and retrojective prophecy. If I say now that on the first of January in a specific year in the future I will have a heart attack, and it happens, that is a projective prophecy. If I were to have (this is a horrible example) a heart attack today and say to myself in the hospital bed (let's give me the benefit of survival in this hypothetical example), "Ah, that's what that pain was last week and the week before," that's retrojective prophecy. That's going back *after the fact* and seeing the future in the past. This is what I mean by prophecy here. It's not as if everyone was reading this text and waiting for, say, a virgin birth. This is retrojective prophecy, going back after the fact and selecting a certain text and saying, "See!" Whenever I speak of prophecy today, I'll be talking about retrojective prophecy.

We talked about the virgin birth in both Matthew and Luke. But notice that Luke never explicitly mentions Isaiah, so if we didn't have Matthew, we might miss the Isaiah prophecy completely. But Matthew and Luke use the same phrase, almost verbatim. In Matthew 1:21, "The child conceived in her is from the Holy Spirit. She will bear a son, and you are to name him Jesus." In Luke 1:31, "You will conceive in your womb and bear a son, and you will name him Jesus." For two independent sources, such as Matthew and Luke here, this requires some explanation. Matthew explicitly quotes Isaiah, and Luke implicitly. How did that happen?

You shouldn't assume that all early Christian tradition viewed Isaiah 7:14 as prophesying a virginal conception of Jesus. In fact, you can't find it anywhere except in Matthew and Luke. But it is a common point, and it tells us something about the tradition prior to Matthew and Luke. Some Christians applied Isaiah 7:14 to Mary's virginal conception.

Once opponents of Christianity heard claims of the virginal conception and divine generation of Jesus, they would reply with instant and obvious rebuttal. No known father means a bastard. The pagan philosopher Celsus, toward the end of the second century, declared in the name of both Judaism and paganism that a cover-up for bastardy must have been the real reason for assertions of the virginal conception of Jesus. The illegitimate father was, he claims, a Roman soldier named Panthera, in whose name we catch a mocking and reversed (*n* and *r* are reversed) allusion to *parthenos*, the Greek word for the young woman in Isaiah 7:14. That is the first major common element in Matthew 1-2 and Luke 1-2, the virginal birth.

A second one is that Jesus is born in David's village, Bethlehem. Matthew and Luke agree that Jesus was born in Bethlehem, a village south of Jerusalem in the Judean hills. Once again, however, this is mythology rather than history. In the Hebrew Scriptures, according to 1 Samuel 17:12, "David was the son of an Ephrathite of Bethlehem in Judah, named Jesse, who had eight sons." In Israelite tradition, David was much more than a past monarch. He was, like Arthur, the once and future king. As waves of social injustice, foreign domination and colonial exploitation swept across Jewish territory, people imagined, hoped and dreamed of a future Davidic leader who would bring back the peace and glory of a bygone age. This hope was hallowed, of course, by long-standing nostalgia and suffused with utopian idealism. The Davidic monarch is the ideal king who will remedy those evils.

For example, among the prophecies in the book of Micah, a younger contemporary of Isaiah in the late eighth century B.C.E., in verse 5:2, "But you, O Bethlehem of Ephrathah, who are one of the little clans of Judah, from you shall come forth for me one who is to rule in Israel whose origin is from of old, from ancient days." Once again we have the same thing in Matthew 2:5-6, where we have an explicit quotation of Micah 5:2. In Luke 2:4,11 we have only an implicit quotation of Micah 5:2. Both Matthew and Luke have to have Jesus born in Bethlehem in order to fulfill Micah 5:2.

How does Luke do it? Well, you know the story in Luke 2:1-6: "In those days, a decree went out from Emperor Augustus that all the world should be registered. This was the first registration that was taken while Quirinius was governor of Syria. All went to their own towns to be registered. Joseph also went from the town of Nazareth in Galilee to Judea, to the city of David called Bethlehem, because he was descended from the house and family of David. He went to be registered with Mary, to whom he was engaged and who was expecting a child. While they were there, the time came for her to deliver her child."

There are three problems with this story. And I really hate to do this because it is a marvelous story. Remember that we have to get Jesus born in Bethlehem.

First, of course, there was no worldwide census under Octavius Augustus. Second, there was indeed a census in Judea, Samaria and Idumea, the territories formally ruled by Herod the Great's son Archelaus, when the Romans exiled him to Gaul and annexed his lands in 6 C.E. But 6 C.E. is about ten years after the death of Herod. Publius Sulpicius Quirinus, the imperial legate for Syria in 6-7 B.C.E., would have been in charge of that census, and of course he would only have done it once, ten years after the death of Herod the Great. Third, why did the Romans take a census? Did they just like to count? They took a census for taxation purposes. They wanted to know where you were so they could get your money. We know from census records in Egypt under Roman law that if you left your home you had to tell the authorities that you had left. But now think for a moment of the administrative nightmare imagined by Luke. Everyone goes back to where they were born to register and then returns to wherever they work. That, in the first century, just as in the 20th century, would be a bureaucratic nightmare. (I shouldn't make any cracks about Washington, should I?)

The story is pure fiction. It's a marvelous story if you don't think about it. But I'm not mocking Luke. I wouldn't dare mock a story that has lasted for 2,000 years and hasn't been picked apart by most people. Most people don't ask how such a census would facilitate taxation. The simple fact is that Jesus' story begins in Nazareth and Luke has to get him to Bethlehem to be born. Matthew, by the way, doesn't have the same problem. He starts the story as if they were living in Bethlehem. He seems to take it for granted they were living there originally and only afterwards had to leave because of Archelaus.

Notice, by the way, once again, that only Matthew and Luke seem to know this material. For example, in John 7, where they're arguing about whether or not Jesus is the Messiah, "Others said, 'This is the Messiah.' But some asked, 'Surely the Messiah does not come from Galilee, does he? Has not the scripture said that the Messiah is descended from David and comes from Bethlehem, the village where David lived?' " You can imagine, if John knew Jesus was born in Bethlehem, the marvelous put-down he could have used there: "But he was born in Bethlehem. Gotcha!"

There is no indication anywhere else in the New Testament that anyone thinks Jesus was born in Bethlehem. Understand very clearly what this means. That Jesus was born of a virgin is told in a story that fulfills Isaiah 7:14. That Jesus was born in Bethlehem is told in a story that fulfills Micah 5:2. What we are interested in is the fulfillment of prophecy. But, it looks like prophecy is the force creating the story. We know Jesus was born; that is the best way to start your life. But then, some of us want to go back into the past and tell the story in the light of that past, as the fulfillment of our ancient scriptures.

The Basic Level: Augustus and Jesus. I'm now down to the third level, which is for me the most important one. Everything I have said so far seems negative. That's what I hear from my undergraduate students when they plan to go home and bug their parents by telling them that there were no Magi.

Yes. On the negative side, I am saying there was no journey to Bethlehem, there was no birth in the stable, there was no presentation in the Temple, and there was certainly no put-down of the teachers in the Temple when Jesus was 12; there was no massacre of infants, there were no Magi, no star, and there was no flight into Egypt. That's all negative. But I've tried to put all this in a positive framework so you can see what those writers intended to emphasize.

Second, there is the virginal birth and the Bethlehem birth. Let me focus on the virginal conception just to show what is positive and what is negative. If you ask me if the virginal conception should be taken literally or metaphorically, I would say metaphorically. It is not a literal statement about the biology of Mary. It is a credal statement about the status of Jesus. In a certain sense, that whole debate—about the literal or metaphorical and the biology of Mary—misses the point completely. And I don't mean the point just for the 20th century. I mean the point for the first century, too. I think if we had Luke and Matthew here and we got into that debate, that's what they'd tell us: "You're missing the point."

So what is the point? What is the real question? Forget Jesus for a moment, and go back 40 years and cross the Mediterranean to a different shore and come to Rome. Julius Caesar has just returned engorged with the spoils and slaves of Gaul in 46 B.C.E. He buys a large piece of land at the northwest corner of the ancient Roman forum, and there he builds and consecrates his own forum, which is said to be more beautiful than the old one, which had grown without any overall plan. In his new forum he puts a temple, the temple to Venus Genetrix, Venus, my ancestress, my mom Venus.

Watch very carefully. Watch how the religious and the political are totally and inextricably intertwined here. Venus

Genetrix. The Julian gens, the Julian family, claims that, at the time of the Trojan War, Aphrodite, or Venus (different names, same goddess), and Anchises produced Aeneas, from whom the Julian tribe descended. Julius Caesar claims to be descended from a goddess, from a divine and human conjunction. Imagine Cassius and Brutus having a discussion about that. Cassius says, "You know I really think, Brutus, the big question is if we should take this literally or metaphorically. That really bothers me, Brutus." And Brutus says, "Cassius, go count the daggers." Cassius: "But is it literal or is it metaphorical?" Brutus: "You do have a lean and hungry look. Go count the daggers."

In one sense, of course, the claim of divine origin is to be taken metaphorically. And I don't even know how they took it, to be honest. Maybe they took it literally, and maybe they took it metaphorically. I know they took it seriously. And I don't think anyone was laughing. So Caesar died two years later. Julius Caesar and of course Augustus and the Julian-Claudian dynasty are descended from a goddess and a human man. Over against that we have the story of Jesus descended from God and a human woman.

Is there any validity to putting those two things together? Let me give you two arguments. The first argument is this. There is extant a decree of calendrical change for the Roman province of Asia. It's on marble stelae in the Asian temples dedicated to the Roman Empire and Augustus and dates to around 9 C.E. "Whereas Providence...has...adorned our lives with the highest good, Augustus...and has in her beneficence granted us and those who have come after us [a *Savior*] who has made war to cease and who shall put everything [in *peaceful*] order, with the result that the *birthday* of our *God* signals the beginning of *good news* for the world because of him....Therefore...the Greeks in Asia decreed that the New Year begin for all the cities on September 23...and the first month...be observed as the month of Caesar, beginning...,"[2] etc., etc.

Notice the key words (my italics). And listen once again to what the angels say to the shepherds in the fields near Bethlehem. Forget for the moment whether it actually happened or not, and just listen to the words. "But the angel said to them, 'Do not be afraid; for see—I am bringing you *good news* of great joy for all the people: to you is *born* this day in the city of David a *Savior*, who is the Messiah, the Lord....Glory to *God* in the highest heaven, and on earth *peace* among those whom he favors!'" (Luke 2:10-11,14). We begin to catch a glimpse of the real question here. It's not about the biology of Mary. It is where God is manifested for you. Is it in the peasant Jesus or the imperial Augustus?

A second argument, to confirm that I'm not just imagining this from a 20th-century point of view. Sometime between 177 and 180 C.E., when the emperor Marcus Aurelius was already persecuting Christians, Celsus, whom I mentioned earlier, wrote his *On the True Doctrine* as an intellectual attack on Christianity. When Celsus discusses Jesus' virgin birth, for example, he never says such an event is incredible in itself. He would never say that. He knows too many stories about similar events from his own pagan tradition. What is incredible to him is that it could happen to a member of the lower classes, a Jewish peasant nobody like Jesus. That blows his mind. Here are his words: "What absurdity! Clearly the Christians have used the myths of the Danae and the Melanippe, or of the Auge and the Antiope, in fabricating the story of Jesus' virgin birth....After all, the old myths of the Greeks that attribute divine birth to Perseus, Amphion, Aeneas and Minos are equally good evidence of their wondrous works on behalf of mankind—and are certainly no less lacking in plausibility than the stories of your followers. What have you done by word or deed that is quite so wonderful as those heroes of old?"[3]

That's the objection. It is not absurd in Celsus' mind to claim that Jesus was *divine*. It is absurd to claim that *Jesus* was divine. Who is he, or what has he done to deserve such a birth? Class snobbery is in fact very close to the root of that objection. Let me confirm it again by quoting him. "First, however, I must deal with the matter of Jesus, the so-called savior, who not long ago taught new doctrines and was thought to be a son of God. This savior, I shall attempt to show, deceived many and caused them to accept a form of belief harmful to the well-being of mankind. Taking its root in the lower classes, the religion continues to spread among the vulgar: Nay one can even say it spread because of its vulgarity and the illiteracy of its adherents. And while there are a few moderate, reasonable and intelligent people who are inclined to interpret its beliefs allegorically, yet it thrives in its purer form among the ignorant."

In summary, then, it is not enough to keep saying that Jesus was not born of a virgin, was not born of David's lineage, was not born in Bethlehem, that there were no stables, no shepherds, no star, no Magi, no massacre of the infants, no flight into Egypt. All of that I think is absolutely true. But it still begs the real question, which is, then as now, where *you* find the divine manifest on this earth. Is it in Caesar, or is it in Jesus? Is it in imperial grandeur or peasant poverty? Is it in domination and subjugation of others from the top down, or is it in the empowerment and liberation of others from the bottom up? That's the real question.

ENDNOTES

1. For this comparison of Matthew 1-2 on Jesus' birth and the popular versions of Exodus 1-2 on Moses' birth, see my article, "From Moses to Jesus: Parallel Themes," *Bible Review* 2:2 (1986), pp. 18-27. But note especially my indebtedness to the work of Renée Bloch, cited in the first footnote on page 27.

2. Frederick W. Danker, *Benefactor: Epigraphic Study of a Graeco-Roman and New Testament Semantic Field* (St. Louis: Clayton Publishing House, 1982), n. 33, pp. 215-222.

3. Celsus, *On the True Doctrine,* trans. R. Joseph Hoffman (New York: Oxford University Press, 1987).

QUESTIONS & ANSWERS

What was Luke's intent when he wrote the Gospel? Why did he fabricate this mythological construct of Jesus? What did he have to gain by doing this, and why did he write what he did?

As clearly as I can see, Luke is taking on Augustus and the myth of the divine Roman emperor. In case the reader missed it, he mentions Augustus just before he mentions his announcement to the angels. I think Luke's intent is to ask exactly this question. Where you are going to find your God? He says *we're* going to find him in a peasant born of God, a peasant who is both divine and human. Now I think we can't hear that today because we go religious. We ask if that can happen. And then we debate whether it could or could not happen. We debate, let's call it, a religious question.

But Luke is a political-religious manifesto. I don't want to say it's political as against religious because, in the first century, no one could make that distinction. How could you make the distinction for Julius Caesar's forum and temple of Venus and say what's political about them and what's religious? Luke is taking on the Roman Empire. It's the beginning of the knock-down battle between Christianity and the Roman Empire. That's what he's up to, and I think he's doing it quite, quite consciously. I think if Luke were here today, at least until I got to the third layer, he'd be saying, "He doesn't get it, he doesn't get it. He really doesn't get it." I hope by the time I got to my third level, he'd know that I had begun to see the point. We're taking on Caesar.

I'm curious what, if anything, from a historical perspective, we know or have figured out. When was Jesus born? Who were his parents? Where was he born? Herod existed, I know that. But you said there was no slaughter, and the census was much later. So I'm curious about what we can pinpoint historically.

Here is my historical reconstruction. At Nazareth, Jesus is born in the normal way human beings are born, to parents called Mary and Joseph. I do not think he was necessarily the firstborn son. If Mary was a virgin and had other children, he would have to be the firstborn son. I have no reason to think that because I do not take the virgin birth literally. He may well have been the youngest son. It would make more sense to me, in a way, if James was the eldest. We know of four brothers and of at least two sisters. So at least a family of seven children and two parents. My understanding is that Joseph probably died young (presumably from exhaustion).

When was Jesus born? Can we be sure it was during the reign of Herod? That gives us around 33 years from which to choose. Can we be certain he died towards the end of the reign of Herod? No. Luke mentions Herod and Matthew mentions Herod, but they're in a very tendentious situation, and it could be part of their story lines. I'd put "born under Herod" with lots of question marks. We're certain when Jesus died, under Pontius Pilate, which gives us a range of ten years, 26-36 C.E. We are not certain he was born under Herod, which means we are not certain he was 30 years of age.

By the way, it is not surprising that we know nothing about the birth of Jesus. We tend to know when people are killed, and then we go back and try to find out about their infancy or when they were born, and we find out nobody really knows. It would be very surprising, actually, if we really knew when Jesus was born. I would say we do not know and we should not presume we know the date of Jesus' birth, and we should not, therefore, presume we know his age when he died. But we are absolutely certain that Jesus died under Pontius Pilate. I would say, historically, that is as sure as anything in history ever gets. No such security attaches to any date or time for Jesus' birth.

Would it be fair to conclude that Matthew and Luke, in writing their accounts of the virginal conception of Jesus, intended to say nothing whatever about human sexuality?

If we explore virginal conception a little more, we're probably going to get into the patriarchal questions that Marcus Borg raised earlier. I don't think virginal conception is a totally innocent statement. It is unfortunate that Mediterranean culture is very good on virgins and mothers and not so good on anything in between, like wives, lovers and friends. But it is very good on the two extremes, and in virginal conception we have brought the two extremes together. I am afraid it does carry prejudices from patriarchal culture with it. It's not innocent, and it has not been innocent, certainly, in 2,000 years in the way it has been handled.

I got the message twice, once from Hershel Shanks and once from you, that the Christ of faith and the Jesus of history are two different things. But if they are, then the Christ of faith must be false because, if the Christ of faith is based on the

Jesus of history, and if they are different, then doesn't that rule out the Christ of faith, even though there is a Christ of faith?

I would never make that distinction. You did not hear that distinction made by me. Here's what I imagine. If you were in Galilee, let's say, in the 30s, you would have seen a person called Jesus. Let's imagine three different people responding to that person. One says, "This guy's a bore. Let's leave him." The second one says, "This guy's dangerous. Let's kill him." The third one says, "I see God here. Let's follow this guy."

Now, each of these, in its own way, is an act of faith. The Romans who said to kill him were making an act of faith in the Roman order. But I'm going to call it "Christian faith," for want of a better name, with quotation marks around it, when some people looked at Jesus in the hills of Galilee in the 30s or whenever and said, "Here is where I see God." They *may* also have been saying that we don't see God in the Temple, or maybe we don't see God in the Torah, and we certainly don't see God in the Roman peace. Maybe if you see God in Jesus, that's a very dangerous situation. That's an act of faith at that very moment. It's not an act of faith in Jesus, it's an act of faith in Jesus *as the manifestation of God.* You cannot make an act of faith in a fact. Jesus is a fact. He's just there. But to say that here is where I see God is an act of faith.

For me you never have an act of faith unless you're talking about (1) a divine referent (2) in material manifestation (3) for a believer. If everyone yawned when Jesus talked, first of all we wouldn't be talking about him now, and he would not be the Son of God. Somebody has to say, "I believe." No, it's not the Jesus of history against the Christ of faith. I just won't accept that distinction. The distinction is, when you look at Jesus, do you see God, that is, a manifestation of God, or do you not. That was the question in the first century, and that is the question in the 20th century. And the clearest evidence is that people could go either way. They did not find Jesus so compelling that they just had to believe.

My answer is that Christian faith is to see the historical Jesus *as* the manifestation of God *for* me. The dichotomy between the Jesus of history and the Christ of faith comes out of Protestant theology. I am coming out of Roman Catholic theology, so I have a whole different set of prejudices.

IV. PORTRAITS
OF JESUS

The title of this lecture is "Portraits of Jesus." It's clear, if you look at the sequence of talks, that my task is also to cover the public life of Jesus. Dom Crossan talked about the birth narratives earlier and will talk about the death and Easter narratives in the last lecture. I get to do the in-between. Of course the in-between is enormous. It's all the public activity of Jesus as an adult. It's the whole question of what his message and his mission were about.

I will begin by talking about two widespread portraits of Jesus, the first one popular and the second one scholarly. Second, I will describe six contemporary scholarly portraits of Jesus, all done by North American scholars in the past decade. And third and finally, I will talk briefly about where I think we are in the discipline, elements about which there is some consensus and elements about which there continue to be division and uncertainty.

I begin by describing two widespread images or portraits of Jesus. One is popular, the one that has dominated the Christian imagination throughout most of the Christian centuries. The second is scholarly, namely the one that has dominated much of this century's scholarship until recently.

By the popular image of Jesus, I mean simply the most widespread image. Its answers to the three central questions about Jesus, his identity, his mission and his message, are clear and direct. Who was he according to this popular image? He was the divinely begotten Son of God. His mission or his purpose? His intention was to die for the sins of the world. His message was about many things but primarily about himself—about who he was, what his purpose was and the importance of believing in him.

This is the image of Jesus that I grew up with within the church, and this is how most people who have heard anything at all about Jesus, whether they are Christian or non-Christian, think of him. It is the most widespread image of Jesus around, whether people believe it to be true or not. This image, of course, is crystallized in what may be the best known verse in the whole of the New Testament, John 3:16. It's the verse that is held up behind the goal posts during field goal attempts at NFL football games. Many of you know it by heart: "For God so loved the world that he gave his only begotten son that whosoever believes in him should not perish, but have everlasting life." There you have the popular image, Jesus as the Son of God given for the sake of the world. Believe in him and you may have everlasting life. To crystallize this popular image of Jesus down to two words, this is essentially an image of Jesus as the "divine savior."

Very importantly, this image of Jesus is not seen by mainstream scholars as a historical image. This is not what Jesus was like as a figure of history. To explain that a bit further, I want to say something about where this popular image of Jesus comes from. It comes from a surface reading of the Gospels, reading them as if they were straightforward historical documents. In particular, the popular image is largely the product of reading all the Gospels through the lens of John's Gospel and of later Christian tradition, including the creeds.

Through this lens, Jesus is seen as one who proclaimed himself with the most exalted titles known in his day. In John's Gospel, for example, are all of the great "I am" statements: "I am the light of the world" (8:12, 9:5, 12:46), "I am the bread of life" (6:35,48-51,58), "I am the resurrection and the life" (11:25), "I am the way, the truth and the life" (14:6) and so forth. He is "the word made flesh" (1:14) according to John. If you add to that the Christian creeds, he becomes a divine figure.

One of the most certain results of the quest for the historical Jesus is that John is not historical. Jesus never talked like this. By the way, this was one of the first things I learned in my very first seminary course almost 30 years ago. It seemed important but also vaguely scandalous and something I shouldn't tell my mother. And I don't think I ever did!

An important qualification—to say that John is not historical does not mean that John is simply wrong or worthless. Rather, when we understand John's Gospel for what it is, it is very powerful. But as an accurate historical account, it is deeply misleading. Let me explain that a bit further with a distinction between two phrases I think are very helpful, the pre-Easter Jesus and the post-Easter Jesus.

By the first of those phrases, the pre-Easter Jesus, I mean, of course, the historical Jesus, Jesus as a figure of history before his death, Jesus as a flesh-and-blood Galilean Jew who was probably about five feet tall. (We don't actually know how tall he was, but that was the average height of males at that time in that culture.) That's the pre-Easter Jesus.

By the phrase post-Easter Jesus, which may be less familiar, I mean the Jesus of Christian tradition and experience. That is, after his death, the followers of Jesus, both in the first century and, I would say, to this day, continue to experience him as a living spiritual reality with qualities traditionally ascribed to God. That's the post-Easter Jesus. The post-Easter Jesus is Jesus as the living, risen Christ of Christian experience and tradition.

John's Gospel is basically about the post-Easter Jesus. Why does the author of John say that Jesus is the light of the world? Because the community out of which John's Gospel comes and for which John's Gospel was written had experienced the risen, living Christ as the light that brought them out of darkness.

Similarly, why, if Jesus never said "I am the bread of life," does John's Gospel have him talk that way? Again, because the community out of which that Gospel comes had experienced the living spiritual Christ as the spiritual food that fed them on their journey to that day.

So John's Gospel is basically about the post-Easter Jesus. The popular image of Jesus is generated by reading the Gospels through the lens of the post-Easter Jesus.

This popular image is not an accurate image of the pre-Easter Jesus. To summarize and put it bluntly in three quick statements as I'm going to may seem almost brutal. In all likelihood, the pre-Easter Jesus did not think of himself as the Messiah or in any of the exalted terms in which he is spoken of. Second, we can say with almost complete certainty that he did not see his own mission or purpose as dying for the sins of the world. Third and finally, again with almost complete certainty, we can say that his message was not about himself or the importance of believing in him.

If that isn't what he was like, then what was he like? I turn now to another widespread image of Jesus, this one from scholarly circles. This was the dominant scholarly image of Jesus in 20th-century scholarship until recently. Made famous by Albert Schweitzer at the beginning of this century, it's a portrait of Jesus as an eschatological prophet or an eschatological figure.

The key to this portrait of Jesus is the definition of the technical term eschatology. The word eschatology means "last things," or "having to do with last things." The word *eschaton* means the final event or the end times. Within a Jewish framework, eschatology refers to the coming of the messianic age, the end-time events brought about by a dramatic act of God typically involving such features as the resurrection of the dead, the last judgment and the dawn of the everlasting kingdom. It is concerned with the end of the world but not the end of the physical earth or the universe, the space-time world. In Jewish eschatologies, the space-time earth, or the space-time universe, frequently survives in a renewed kind of way. Nevertheless, the change is so dramatic that one may, at least metaphorically, speak of eschatology as being concerned with the end of the world.

Understanding Jesus as an eschatological prophet means understanding that the conviction that the end-times were at hand was central to him. This is what Jesus meant when he said, "The kingdom of God is at hand" (Mark 1:15; Matthew 4:17). He was referring to the imminent *eschaton*, the imminent arrival of the end-times. When he spoke of the coming of the Son of Man on the clouds of heaven—I am referring to how this was seen at the beginning of this century—he was referring to the coming of a supernatural figure who would rule over the everlasting kingdom, either someone other than himself or himself in a transformed state (Mark 13:26; Matthew 24:30).

For this image of Jesus, the conviction that the end was at hand was not peripheral. Rather, it was at the center of Jesus' understanding, message and mission. Indeed, it is where his message of repentance got its urgency. Time is short, so repent.

This view, foreign as it is to many people, in fact dominated the mainstream of Jesus scholarship in both Germany and North America through the middle third of this century. There was a virtual scholarly consensus that Jesus was an eschatological figure in the sense that I have just described. This is what I have called elsewhere the eschatological consensus. That consensus, very importantly, has now collapsed. There are still scholars who affirm it, but as a consensus, it's gone. I won't go through the reasons why, even though it's one of the most exciting developments of the last 15 years or so. Rather, I'll simply quote Professor James Robinson of the Claremont School of Theology, one of the senior New Testament scholars in North America. In a talk given in Vienna a couple of years ago, Robinson spoke of the collapse of the eschatological consensus as "the fading of apocalyptic, and a paradigm shift and Copernican revolution in the discipline. The eschatological image of Jesus is an old model which is frayed and blemished with broken parts, a procrustean bed in which the discipline squirms."[1] The collapse of the eschatological consensus is one of the central characteristics of the renaissance of historical Jesus scholarship. It's one of the central reasons that the question of what Jesus was like as a figure of history has arisen anew.

This leads me to the second main section of this talk, the six portraits of Jesus in contemporary North American biblical scholarship.

SIX PORTRAITS OF JESUS	
Portrait Type	*Author*
Restoration Eschatology Prophet	Sanders
Hellenistic-type Cynic Sage	Mack
Egalitarian Wisdom Prophet	Schüssler Fiorenza
Social Prophet	Horsley
Spirit Person	Borg
Jewish Cynic Peasant	Crossan

I begin first with the work of E. P. Sanders. Sanders' work represents the most direct continuation of the eschatological consensus in North American scholarship. The book in which he works this out, *Jesus and Judaism*,[2] published in 1985, has been highly acclaimed. The *New York Times* book reviewer at the time of publication said it was likely to be the most important book of the decade in the discipline. At the end of the decade, it won the prestigious and financially very rewarding Grawemeyer Award as the best book of the decade in religious studies.

In that book Sanders develops a picture of Jesus as a prophet and agent of Jewish restoration eschatology. The key to understanding that somewhat technical-sounding mouthful is in the last two words, restoration eschatology. Restoration eschatology is an understanding of the end-times that emphasizes the restoration of Israel in fulfillment of God's promises. This, Sanders argues, was a central theme of Judaism in the post-Exilic period, which began with the return of the exiles from Babylonia in 539/8 B.C.E.

Restoration eschatology refers to the coming of the messianic age (although it wouldn't necessarily involve an individual known as the Messiah), a time of deliverance. Specifically, it would include four elements. It would involve the ingathering of the 12 tribes of Israel. It would be centered in Jerusalem; Mount Zion would be the center of the messianic age. Third, it often involved a new or renewed Temple. And fourth, it would involve a new social order. All of this was to be established by God through direct divine intervention. Restoration eschatology meant the end of the present age and the dawn of the new age.

According to Sanders, this is what Jesus expected, and he expected it soon. The proper framework for interpreting the traditions about Jesus, Sanders argues, is the interpretative framework of restoration eschatology.

It's important to note how concrete, literal in a sense, Sanders' account of Jesus' expectation is. For example, Jesus believed that there really would be a new or renewed Temple in Jerusalem. This is not a metaphor. Moreover, Jesus' action of overturning tables in the Temple symbolized, Sanders argues, the coming destruction of the Temple and its replacement by a new or renewed Temple. Moreover, Jesus believed that he and the Twelve would rule over the restored Israel from the new Temple in Jerusalem, all within the framework of the space-time world. And finally, Jesus may even have thought of himself as the king or soon-to-be king of the coming kingdom.

Sanders works all of this out in great detail. Thus, for Sanders, Jesus was both a prophet and an agent of restoration eschatology. He spoke about it, and he worked to bring it about. The continuity with Schweitzer's understanding of Jesus is striking. Indeed, Sanders' is the only one of the six portraits that I'll be talking about that continues the eschatological consensus.

The second portrait comes from Burton Mack of Claremont Graduate School, and it's a picture of Jesus as a Hellenistic-type cynic sage. It's developed in Mack's two books, *A Myth of Innocence*[3] and *The Lost Gospel*.[4] Burton Mack does not really regard himself as a Jesus scholar but more of a gospel scholar, Markan scholar and "Q" scholar. Mack is also the North American scholar most associated with the cynic image of Jesus. So whether he likes to regard himself as a Jesus scholar or not, he's in the group. In his 1988 book, what he calls a softly focused characterization of Jesus emerges.

Before I describe what the phrase "Hellenistic-type cynic sage" means, I want to speak briefly about how Mack arrives at this image of Jesus. His first claim is that the earliest layer of the Jesus tradition, which would be the earliest layer of the Q document that Steve Patterson spoke about, is a wisdom text that portrays Jesus as a teacher of wisdom and contains short sayings and a few parables. Everything else in the Gospels, Mack argues, is later. Everything eschatological or apocalyptic is later; conflict material is later and so forth. So the earliest layer is a wisdom layer.

The second major ingredient grounding Mack's portrait is a picture of a deeply Hellenized Galilee, where the process of becoming more and more cosmopolitan had gone very far indeed. Mack is even skeptical that there were synagogues in Galilee. He thinks there were cynic sages present in Galilee. Thus an image of Jesus as a cynic sage would be at home in the Galilean environment.

What portrait of Jesus emerges from this? A portrait of a Hellenistic-style cynic sage. The phrase suggests, first of all, an itinerant teacher, without a home, on the road, one who has deliberately abandoned the world by becoming homeless. As such, Jesus taught a kind of wisdom that mocked or subverted conventional beliefs. Jesus was a scoffer, a gadfly, a debunker who could playfully or sarcastically or with considerable charm ridicule the conventions and preoccupations that animated and imprisoned most people. He was like a Jewish Socrates, if you will, but a Socrates who has become homeless.

Mack's image of Jesus is really the polar opposite of Ed Sanders' image of Jesus. For Sanders, Jesus is deeply eschatological and deeply Jewish. For Burton Mack, Jesus is not eschatological and not very Jewish. Mack agrees he's Jewish by birth. But the adult Jesus is not concerned with Jewish institutions and not concerned with the future of the Jewish people. He is a highly individualistic Hellenistic-style cynic sage.

The third portrait comes from Elisabeth Schüssler Fiorenza, the most influential feminist New Testament scholar in North America. In her 1983 book, *In Memory of Her*,[5] she brings a feminist perspective to her reading of texts. As a feminist scholar, she is especially sensitive to the two related but not identical phenomena I talked about earlier, namely androcentrism and patriarchy. From her reading of the texts with these sensitivities, a picture of Jesus as an egalitarian, anti-patriarchal wisdom prophet emerges. To begin with the last phrase first, in common with many contemporary scholars, she sees Jesus as a wisdom figure, that is, a teacher who used characteristic wisdom forms of speech, such as parables and aphorisms.

In addition, and this is what makes her portrait distinctive, she points out that the gospels sometimes portray Jesus as speaking on behalf of wisdom or as a child of wisdom. In Luke 11:49, for example, the Jesus of Luke says, "Therefore the wisdom of God said...." Then Jesus speaks, and, for our purposes, what he says isn't as important as the fact that he is represented as speaking on behalf of the wisdom of God.

Wisdom in Jewish wisdom literature is often personified as a woman. The Greek word for wisdom, which is also a woman's name in English and therefore works nicely, is *sophia*, so that scholars often speak of wisdom in Jewish wisdom literature personified as Sophia. In that same literature, wisdom is often spoken of as the functional equivalent of God. Wisdom is spoken of as having been present with God at creation. Wisdom, or Sophia, is spoken of as the agent of creation, as present in the world, and has many divine attributes. Thus, in Jewish wisdom literature, wisdom, or Sophia, sometimes functions as a female image of God. Even in the biblical tradition we find elements of Jewish wisdom literature.

When Jesus refers to himself as the spokesperson of wisdom, he speaks of himself as the spokesperson of Sophia, or maybe even the child of Sophia. Sophia is the name of Israel's god personified in female form. This is what Schüssler Fiorenza means when she says that Jesus was a wisdom prophet. He was a prophet of divine Sophia.

The other phrase in that shorthand telegram message characterizing Schüssler Fiorenza's portrait of Jesus is egalitarian and anti-patriarchal. As a prophet of Sophia, Jesus rejected the purity and patriarchy system of his day and carried out his mission to the marginalized members of society in the name of an alternative vision of human community. That vision, Schüssler Fiorenza says, was embodied in the egalitarian praxis of the kingdom of God, which she understands as a discipleship of equals. Jesus' egalitarian praxis subverted the major divisions of his social world, divisions between pure and impure, healthy and maimed, male and female. Thus there is a very strong sociopolitical dimension to Schüssler Fiorenza's understanding of Jesus.

The fourth portrait is by Richard Horsley, one of the most prolific North American New Testament scholars in recent years. He is the author of *Bandits, Prophets, and Messiahs*,[6] *The Liberation of Christmas*,[7] *Sociology and the Jesus Movement*[8] and

Jesus and the Spiral of Violence.[9] In *Jesus and the Spiral of Violence,* Horsley develops a picture of Jesus as an Elijah-style social prophet and community organizer. The framework for this portrait is the centrality that Horsley gives to the study of peasant societies in his analysis of the Jesus traditions and to the conflict between urban ruling elites and rural peasants.

Within this framework, Jesus emerges first as an Elijah-type social prophet. The reference, of course, is to the prophet Elijah, a ninth-century B.C.E. figure of ancient Israel who protested against the ruling elites of his day and fomented a social revolution. As a social prophet in the tradition of Elijah, Jesus was passionate about the injustices of the peasant agrarian society of his time. He challenged and indicted the ruling elites and their retainers.

As a community organizer, Jesus sought to reorganize village society into relatively autonomous self-sufficient communities of solidarity. This is the context in which Horsley puts some of the most familiar sayings of Jesus, sayings about lending without question, about giving without worrying about return, sayings about the mutual forgiveness of debts— all of which refer to the reorganization of village life. Horsley points out, as many other scholars have, that the original wording of the Lord's Prayer is "forgive us our debts, as we forgive our debtors." We've always taken that as a metaphor for trespasses, but Horsley says, in the context of a peasant society, it was probably meant literally—don't hold your indebted neighbor responsible for his debt. That's what the forgiveness of debts means.

Importantly for Horsley, Jesus sought to bring about a social revolution but not a political revolution. The distinction is significant; social revolution starts at the bottom and moves up, and political revolution starts at the top and moves down. A political revolution is intended to change the governing class. Jesus, Horsley argues, was concerned about inaugurating a social revolution; he was not seeking to seize "top down" control of power.

Fifth, I turn to a quick sketch of my own understanding of Jesus. It is found in my *Conflict, Holiness and Politics in the Teachings of Jesus*,[10] *Jesus, A New Vision*,[11] *Meeting Jesus Again for the First Time*[12] and *Jesus in Contemporary Scholarship*.[13] Like other scholars, I have written hundreds of pages about this, so it's hard to fit into two and one-half minutes here, but I will try. The best way to crystallize my understanding of Jesus is to see it as a sketch that has four major strokes, each stroke corresponding to a type of religious personality known cross-culturally as well as within the Jewish tradition.

The first stroke is the most important one and the one that, perhaps, most distinguishes my understanding of Jesus. That first stroke is understanding Jesus as a "spirit person." Spirit person is a newly coined technical phrase for a type of religious personality that has been known for a long time.

Spirit persons have two primary defining qualities. They have vivid and frequent experiences of another level or layer of reality, which I refer to as the realm of spirit or the realm of God. They have frequent mystical experiences, if you will, although the word mystical is so misunderstood today that I'm not sure how useful it is. Second, by virtue of these experiences, a spirit person becomes a mediator or a funnel or a conduit for the power of the spirit to flow into this world. Characteristically spirit people are healers, although the power of the spirit flows into this world in other ways as well.

It seems obvious to me that, if we think there really are people like this (and anthropological studies as well as historical studies of Israel are filled with them), then Jesus, whatever else needs to be said about him, was one of them. To use only slightly different language, he was one of those who knew God, not just somebody who believed strongly in God, but someone who knew God in his own experience. The phrase "knowing God" is in fact a phrase from the Hebrew Bible that refers to a number of people in the Jewish tradition who knew God in this way (Jeremiah 31:34; Hosea 4:1, 5:4, 6:6, 13:4).

The second, third and fourth strokes of my portrait I'll do more quickly because they pick up on themes in other people's work as well. My second stroke is that Jesus was a subversive sage. He was a teacher of wisdom, a particular kind of wisdom that was both subversive and alternative. He subverted conventional wisdom and dominant consciousness and invited his hearers to live by an alternative wisdom.

Third, he was a social prophet, a radical critic of the purity system and, more broadly, of the domination system. I argue that he opposed the politics of purity with what I call a politics of compassion.

And fourth and finally, I see him as a movement founder whose purpose was the transformation of Judaism. That is, he did not intend to establish a new religion but rather to renew or transform his own tradition. The movement that came into existence around him was an inclusive movement that embodied the alternative social vision in his teaching as a wisdom teacher and his message as a social prophet.

The sixth and final contemporary portrait I will describe is the Jesus who emerges in the work of John Dominic Crossan. By the way, I have not told him what I am going to say, so he has neither affected nor censored it. I can only hope it is reasonably accurate.

Dom has been well known in the discipline for about 20 years; much of his early work is on wisdom forms in the teaching of Jesus, namely parables and aphorisms. His 1991 book *The Historical Jesus*[14] is a comprehensive treatment of the historical Jesus, and I think it could be the most significant Jesus book since Albert Schweitzer's at the beginning of this century. In the first 18 months after publication, it sold over 50,000 copies, which is remarkable in the scholarly world, especially for a fairly hefty book of about 500 pages. By the way, Dom has a popular version of his book coming out. He calls it his baby Jesus book although the official title is *Jesus: A Revolutionary Biography*.[15] I've seen it in typescript, and it is also very good.

With these two books, Dom has established himself as the premier Jesus scholar in North America, and I trust that might be worth a free dinner tonight. His book is as important for its method as for its results. His method has two major components. First, he develops a quantifiable way of assessing what is earliest in the Jesus tradition by using an archaeological model. He layers the tradition into four strata, from earliest to latest. Then he counts up the number of attestations of particular sayings or complexes in each layer.

The second element in his methodology is an interdisciplinary approach for interpreting these traditions. This is one of the most striking features of his book. Indeed, his book is the finest and fullest fruition to date of the interdisciplinary character of the renaissance in historical Jesus scholarship. Studies in cultural and social anthropology, medical anthropology, the sociology of colonial protest movements, the dynamics and structure of pre-industrial peasant societies, honor-shame societies, patron-client societies and so forth, run throughout his pages. The book is a gold mine of information and insights and an important resource book.

The portrait of Jesus that emerges is that Jesus was a Jewish cynic peasant with an alternative social vision. The emphasis upon peasant is important in terms of understanding the message and activity of Jesus. His message could not be too "heady"; it had to have something to do with the body. To use a phrase from Dom's baby Jesus book, to take seriously the peasant audience of Jesus means that the message of Jesus could not be "too preachy, teachy or speechy."

In the phrase Jewish cynic, both the adjective and the noun are important. To begin with the noun, Dom suggests that Jesus was both like and unlike Hellenistic cynic teachers. How were they alike? Both taught and enacted ways of shattering convention. Both embodied practice, not just theory, a different way of living, not just a different way of thinking. How were they different? The Hellenistic cynic teachers were urban; they addressed the marketplace, and their teaching was individualistic. Jesus, on the other hand, was rural; he addressed peasants, and there was a much more communitarian dimension to his message.

That last point leads to the alternative social vision of Jesus embodied in his two most characteristic activities, magic and meals. Crossan refers provocatively to Jesus as a magician, which he says he means in a neutral and nonpejorative sense.

A magician is somebody else's healer, someone who heals outside of established religious authority. To do so, of course, subverts religious institutions, just as social banditry subverts political institutions. Unauthorized healing, Crossan suggests, is like religious banditry, outside of the authority structure.

The second most characteristic activity is eating. Crossan refers to the open-table practice of Jesus as open "commensality." Open commensality embodied an alternative social vision. Eating together without regard for social boundaries subverted the deepest social boundaries—between honor and shame, patron and client, female and male, slave and free, rich and poor. Together, magic and meal embodied religious and economic egalitarianism that negated the religious and political hierarchies of the day.

I conclude with some observations about where the discipline is and where we're likely to go. I have four brief comments. First, the eschatological debate is not over. I think a change has occurred, and the balance has tipped in favor of a non-eschatological reading of the Jesus tradition. But I think the debate will continue.

Second, the greatest consensus among contemporary New Testament scholars is about Jesus as a wisdom teacher, a consensus that has emerged in the last 20 years. The most characteristic forms of Jesus' speech as a wisdom teacher are parables (basically short stories) and aphorisms (short sayings), both of which crystallize insight. Aphorisms are great one-liners. I think it's fascinating that one of the most certain things we can know about Jesus is that he was a storyteller and a speaker of great one-liners.

Third, there is an emerging tendency within the discipline to see Jesus as political, at least in the broad sense of the word, as concerned with the shape of society. Four of the six portraits I sketched see Jesus in this way. The claim is not that he was exclusively political but that he was political *and* something else. This is a new concept in the discipline. Most scholars in this century have denied that Jesus was political. If Jesus expected the end of everything, why would he be concerned about the social order? Jesus has most often been understood in highly individualistic terms.

Fourth and finally, a comment about Jesus as a spirit person. Most portraits of Jesus do not address this issue. However, in quite different ways, Dom and I, I think, both make this issue central. In one of his articles, Dom refers to Jesus as presumably having had mystical experiences and that Jesus' understanding of the immediacy of God comes from his mystical experiences.[16] If you combine mystical experience and magic, mystic and healer, you have what I mean by spirit person. Whether this will become a central category, I have no idea. But it seems to me an illuminating category.

I conclude with a brief story that goes back to 1988. I was driving through the rain one October morning about six o'clock to the Portland airport to catch a plane to Atlanta. I was flying to Atlanta for a meeting of the Jesus Seminar, at which we were scheduled to vote upon the Lord's Prayer (which is a bizarre thing to do). As I was driving along thinking about the 50 other scholars from all over the country who were converging on Atlanta to vote on the Lord's Prayer, I was listening to NPR's "Morning Edition." The second lead story on "Morning Edition" that day was about the results of laboratory tests on the Shroud of Turin, which, of course, is the alleged burial shroud of Jesus.

I thought to myself, isn't it amazing that 2,000 years after the death of this Galilean peasant a bunch of us are flying to Atlanta to vote on whether or not he said the Lord's Prayer, and the second lead story in the news is about the Shroud of Turin. It was the same year the movie *The Last Temptation of Christ* had come out in the summer, with considerable furor, and that Jesus had been on the cover of *Time* magazine. I was struck by the fact that Jesus is still in the news.

It is striking that this figure continues to exercise such fascinating power on our intellects and our imaginations. The question will be with us for a long time to come. What was he like? What manner of man was he?

ENDNOTES

1. In a paper delivered to the International Meeting of the Society of Biblical Literature in Vienna, August, 1990. See my essay, "Portraits of Jesus in Contemporary North American Scholarship," *Harvard Theological Review* 84 (1991), p. 2.

2. E.P. Sanders, *Jesus and Judaism* (Philadelphia: Fortress, 1985).

3. Burton Mack, *A Myth of Innocence: Mark and Christian Origins* (Philadelphia: Fortress, 1988).

4. Mack, *The Lost Gospel: The Book of Q and Christian Origins* (HarperSanFrancisco, 1993).

5. Elisabeth Schüssler Fiorenza, *In Memory of Her: A Feminist Theological Reconstruction of Christian Origins* (New York: Crossroad, 1983).

6. Richard Horsley and John S. Hanson, *Bandits, Prophets, and Messiahs* (Minneapolis: Winston, 1985).

7. Horsley, *The Liberation of Christmas* (New York: Crossroad, 1989).

8. Horsley, *Sociology and the Jesus Movement* (New York: Crossroad, 1989).

9. Horsley, *Jesus and the Spiral of Violence* (San Francisco: Harper & Row, 1987).

10. Marcus J. Borg, *Conflict, Holiness and Politics in the Teachings of Jesus* (Lewiston, NY: Edwin Mellen Press, 1984).

11. Borg, *Jesus, A New Vision: Spirit, Culture, and the Life of Discipleship* (San Francisco: Harper & Row, 1987).

12. Borg, *Meeting Jesus Again for the First Time* (HarperSanFrancisco, 1994).

13. Borg, *Jesus in Contemporary Scholarship* (Philadelphia: Trinity Press International, forthcoming).

14. John Dominic Crossan, *The Historical Jesus: The Life of a Mediterranean Jewish Peasant* (HarperSanFrancisco, 1992).

15. Crossan, *Jesus: A Revolutionary Biography* (HarperSanFrancisco, 1994).

16. Crossan, "Materials and Methods in Historical Jesus Research," *Forum* 4:4 (1988), p. 11.

QUESTIONS & ANSWERS

How does Walter Wink's portrayal of Jesus as a radical revolutionary using nonviolent methods to oppose the domination system fit in with what you have said here?

The question is about Walter Wink, another of our colleagues, who portrays Jesus as a social revolutionary strongly opposed to the domination system. I think the chapter in which Wink develops that understanding in the third volume of his trilogy—it's called *Engaging the Powers* (Fortress, 1992)—is probably the finest compact analysis I've ever read of the politics of Jesus. By the domination system, Wink means a combination of the purity system, the patriarchy system, the peasant society system and a few other things as well. I'm not convinced that Jesus was ideologically committed to nonviolence, although I think he was nonviolent. But I think Wink's basic claim, that Jesus radically opposed the domination system of his day and, by extension, the domination system of any day, is very persuasive.

Dr. Borg, as you were summing up your excellent talk, I couldn't help but think that some of us who have spent a long time in the Far East were reminded of the Buddha. Do you have any comment?

The question concerns resemblances between Jesus and the Buddha. I regularly name Jesus and the Buddha as the two major religious figures who most resemble each other. Of course, there are all the differences that two different cultures make, the culture of the South Asian subcontinent and the culture of the Middle East and Judaism in particular. So there are cultural differences between the two of them. I also think Jesus was more sociopolitical than the Buddha. But with regard to enlightenment experience and with regard to Jesus' subversive and alternative wisdom being very much like the Buddha's teaching about the Four Noble Truths, I think there are deep similarities. One way I try to express that is to imagine the Buddha and Jesus meeting sometime. If that were to happen, neither one, I'm convinced, would try to convert the other. They would recognize each other.

I'm wondering, being new to this subject, if these views of Jesus don't reflect more on the 20th century than they do on the first century. I mean, he's sort of a stand-up comedian, a cynic, a sort of new-age mystic. Are we hearing more about the 20th century than the first century?

That's a question we historians have to face all the time. One can only try to be self-aware and self-critical as to the possibility of doing that. The other quick comment I would make is that sometimes the experiences of a particular time lead us to see the past more clearly rather than less clearly. In his book *What Is History?* (Random House, 1967), the English historian E. H. Carr draws a comparison between the work of a historian and a person observing a parade, the parade being the moving process of history. Carr says that the historian can never sit in the bleachers and watch the parade because he or she is also part of the historical procession. As the historical procession winds back and forth, the angle of vision on the past is constantly changing. Now we will always see from our own present, but some presents, I am convinced, enable us to see things that other presents don't. By being as self-aware as possible, we can, to some degree, control how much we project our own interests onto the past. I don't have any interest in Jesus being a peasant reformer. I'd rather he was a middle class guy who drove a Mitsubishi. So I appreciate the comment, and we have to be very much aware of it. But I think we do try to be aware of it.

V. THE PASSION, CRUCIFIXION AND RESURRECTION

I have a short introduction and then three subjects. The three subjects will be the crucifixion, the burial and the resurrection of Jesus.

As my introduction, I ask you to think about what we would know about Jesus if we knew nothing at all from Christian sources. We would know about Jesus from Josephus and Tacitus. They agree on three points. First, there was a movement. Second, the authorities—Tacitus mentions just the Romans, Josephus mentions the higher authorities of the Jews and the Romans—crucified Jesus to stop it. Third, it didn't work, and the movement continued to spread.

Those are three historical facts that I would ask you not to forget. There was a movement, and authorities killed the mover, but now it has spread all over the place.

The Crucifixion of Jesus. My first subject is the passion and crucifixion. I am very much aware of asking your indulgence in summarizing a lot of material. To simplify things, I will give you a sharp thesis and then my arguments for it. This is my thesis on the passion. The detailed, almost hour-by-hour, moment-by-moment, who-said-this who-said-that accounts in Matthew, Mark, Luke and John *are not history memorized but prophecy historicized.* So that's the sharp dichotomy—history memorized or prophecy historicized. We shall see what these mean as we go along.

Let me take a first example, a relatively safe one. It won't bother anyone too much. The case is Jesus' silence during the proceedings or the trials. Jesus is silent when he's questioned by Jewish authorities in Mark 14:31 despite immediately answering in Mark 14:62 and answering without any mention of silence in Luke 22:67a-69 and John 18:20-23. Or again, Jesus is silent while being questioned by Roman authorities in Mark 15:5 despite previously answering in Mark 15:2 and answering without any mention of silence in John 18:34-37. Is Jesus' silence under trial *history memorized* or *prophecy historicized?*

By history memorized, I mean that somebody was there, somebody noted the facts, somebody passed them on and eventually they got written down. What do I mean by prophecy historicized? Somebody, after the death of Jesus, searched the Hebrew Scriptures to see if the Elect One (I use that as a general term) could suffer and die. And they found, for example, Isaiah 53:7, which says, "He was oppressed and he was afflicted, yet he did not open his mouth; like a lamb that is led to the slaughter, and like a sheep that before its shearers is silent, so he did not open his mouth." They then told the story of Jesus' trials to conform to that description read as prophecy (retrojective prophecy, of course).

That is what I mean by prophecy historicized. In a way, once you say Jesus was silent, then you can go on and have him talk, because that's not the point. The point is the fulfillment of prophecy. My thesis is that prophecy is creating the stories. That's a first example, and, as I said, it's a relatively safe one. Nobody will live or die for that one.

Let me take a second example, the case of Jesus' multiplicity of trials. In the Acts of the Apostles 4:24-28, Luke says "Sovereign Lord, who made the heaven and the earth, the sea, and everything in them, it is you who said by the Holy Spirit through our ancestor David, your servant [in Psalm 2:1-2]: 'Why did the Gentiles rage, and the peoples imagine vain things? The kings of the earth took their stand, and the rulers have gathered together against the Lord and against his Messiah.' For in this city, in fact, both Herod and Pontius Pilate, with the Gentiles and the peoples of Israel, gathered together against your holy servant Jesus, whom you anointed, to do whatever your hand and your plan had predestined to take place." Now, look at the various stories about the multiple trials of Jesus before his condemnation.

Realize what I am doing. I want to know if prophecy is creating history or history is creating prophecy, as it were. The Gospel of Peter is a gospel not found in the New Testament, but it is one of those in the database that Steve Patterson talked about earlier. I consider that this gospel contains a source independent of the New Testament. In the Gospel of Peter, the trial of Jesus is one great big proceeding with everyone there. Pilate is there, Herod Antipas is there, and the Jewish judges, presumably not the aristocratic ones but the religious ones, are all there at a joint trial. There's only one trial in the Gospel of Peter at 1:1-2.

In Mark there are two separate trials, one before the high priest in 14:53-65 and another before Pontius Pilate in 15:1-20. And when we get to Luke, there are three trials, one before the high priest in 22:54-71, one before Pontius Pilate in 23:1-5, 13-25 and one before Herod Antipas in 23:6-12. At that point we have run out of authorities to conduct trials. We have separate trials by religious authorities, aristocratic Jewish authorities and Roman authorities. My question is if Psalms 2:1-2, which talks about the Messiah being tried before the nations and the kings, is generating the details of the trials.

My third example, and I am getting into more difficult ones each time, is Jesus as the abused scapegoat. We find in the story of Jesus' trial the motifs that he is spat upon and poked with a reed. In Mark 14:65, on trial before the Jewish authorities, Jesus is *struck* and *spat upon*, and in Mark 15:19, on trial before the Roman authorities, he is *struck with a reed* and *spat upon*. In a way, when you're being put to death by crucifixion, it seems a minor detail if you are spat upon or poked with a reed. Yet why do you have that in the text? Why do soldiers who are just doing their job, however cruel it is, bother to spit on somebody? Why do they poke him with a reed? Where do the reeds come from?

Let's take a look at the Epistle of Barnabas, a document that is not in the New Testament. It's a work of exegesis written towards the end of the first century in which Christians meditate explicitly on Hebrew Scripture, or Old Testament texts, and find them fulfilled in the passion of Jesus. As far as we can see, the author doesn't seem to know any of the canonical Gospels.

He hasn't read the stories. He equates Jesus with the scapegoat from the Jewish Day of Atonement (Yom Kippur). Jesus is the scapegoat who carries away the sins of the people. But he knows not only Leviticus 16, which is where you find the story of the scapegoat. He also knows details that aren't in Leviticus 16 but which we find later in the Mishnah, the codification of Jewish law compiled around 200 C.E. by Judah the Patriarch. It looks like he's actually remembering the ceremony; he's not just reading Leviticus.

Barnabas 7:7 says, "Note what was commanded: 'Take two goats, goodly and alike, and offer them (notice how the type of Jesus is manifested)....And do you all spit on it and goad it, and bind the scarlet wool about its head and let it be cast into the desert.' " Apparently, Barnabas knows, and I would presume that this is probably historically correct, that when the scapegoat was being ushered into the desert, the poor beast was spat upon by the people, not as cruelty to animals, but simply to spit their sins out upon it, to get rid of their sins in a physical sense. And poking the goat with the reed, the ordinary instrument they would have at hand, pushes it on its way. You can hardly imagine a more graphic way of saying I empty my sins onto this beast, and get away from me, beast, into the desert.

Which came first? Was Jesus spat upon and poked with a reed in historical fact, and then did people go looking to find those things in the Old Testament texts? Or did they know about the scapegoat and apply the image to Jesus? I am completely convinced that the line went from the scapegoat to Jesus because those poking reeds make more sense moving in that direction than the reverse. The scapegoat typifies Jesus, who dies "for our sins."

Those are only three examples. To convince you completely, I would have to go through the entire passion account, as I did in my 1988 book *The Cross That Spoke*.[1] But understand my thesis. What you have, hour by hour, moment by moment, Pontius Pilate said this, Jesus said that, the high priest said this, is not, I believe, history remembered and transcribed. Maybe that's possible, but I am not talking about what is possible. I am talking about what is probable in these stories. You should understand this because it's very important. If you asked me under oath in a court of law, *could* this or that have actually happened, I would answer yes to any *could* question. Anything *could* have happened. The question is which is more probable in this case. Are we going from prophecy into history or from history into prophecy? My thesis argues for the former option—prophecy into history.

This is my reconstruction of what happened historically during the passion. The people who were with Jesus fled when he was arrested. Those who fled knew nothing about what happened. They could, of course, imagine a crucifixion. It did not take much imagination in first-century Palestine. Those who knew nothing historically combed the scriptures theologically, that is to say, those who were able to read did. Those who combed the scriptures theologically came up with various types and texts that showed how God's Chosen One could suffer and die and still be God's Chosen One. Out of a medley of such types and texts, an historical story was eventually created, and thereafter we have the story that we all know. That is my thesis with regard to the passion of Jesus. With regard to those detailed and multiplying trials of Jesus, we are dealing not with history memorized but with prophecy historicized.

I would ask you to think for a moment how absolutely, how utterly, how unspeakably unfair it was for early Christian writers, say in the third and fourth centuries, to go back to their Jewish colleagues and say, "Don't you understand, can't you read, won't you understand? Read the text, see how it is fulfilled. How can you deny Jesus was the Messiah? There was darkness at noon in Mark 15:30. Read it as foretold in Amos 8:9." Those Christian polemicists quarried from Jewish quarries the very stones they threw at the Jews. I find that unspeakably unfair. And that is for me what is at stake here. Otherwise you could say, "Well, maybe it's prophecy, maybe it's history, but who cares?" I think it is from prophecy that the history was made. It cannot be used, therefore, to batter the people who made the prophecy and who, with equal right and truth, found it fulfilled in very different ways.

The Burial of Jesus. My second subject is the burial of Jesus. Again I'm going to make a strong thesis and then give you a sort of general argument for it. Jesus was buried, *if he was buried at all*, by the people who crucified him. Watch the argument here because there are jumps. What, with regard to Roman practices, do we know about crucifixion? I'm going to quote from Martin Hengel's book about crucifixion. It's really not a book; it's a series of quotations from Greco-Roman authors about crucifixion. It's a catalogue of horrors, actually. I think we have to get back a little of the horror in the heart of darkness to understand crucifixion. What I'm doing here is not trying to be sensational, but I want everyone at the end of this to smell the horror.

"Among the Romans," says Hengel, "[crucifixion] was inflicted above all on the lower classes, i.e., slaves, violent criminals and the unruly elements in rebellious provinces, not least in Judea. The chief reason for its use was its allegedly supreme efficacy as a deterrent; it was, of course, carried out publicly....It was usually associated with other forms of torture, including at least flogging....By the public display of a naked victim at a prominent place—at a crossroads, in the theater, on high ground, at the place of his crime—crucifixion also represented his uttermost humiliation, which had a numinous dimension to it....Crucifixion was aggravated further by the fact that quite often its victims were never buried. It was a stereotyped picture that the crucified victim served as food for wild beasts and birds of prey. In this way his humiliation was made complete. What it meant for a man in antiquity to be refused burial, and the dishonor which went with it, can hardly be appreciated by modern man."[2]

Think for a second. The Romans had three *summa supplica*, or supreme penalties. What made them supreme was not that they hurt more than anything else. The Romans didn't calculate hurt too much. What made them supreme was that there was nothing left to bury. You were annihilated. One of those penalties was crucifixion; the second was being cast to the beasts in the amphitheater; the third was being burned alive.

What made crucifixion awful is that you were probably not buried. Most of the time you were left on the cross for the dogs and the crows. Try to understand and imagine the place of crucifixion. Think of it as what it was intended to be, a place of state terrorism. Probably the uprights were there all the time. Try and imagine the flies. Try and imagine the prowling dogs. Try and imagine the smell of sweat and blood and urine and excrement. That's why Paul admitted that to preach the crucifixion and the crucified Christ was to announce "the folly" of the cross. That is an older translation—a nice word. "Folly" sounds like some charming eccentricity. But the word in Greek is the root from which we get our word *moronic*. Paul speaks with devastating accuracy of the absolute stupidity in the Roman world of announcing a crucified Christ.

According to Roman practices, therefore, Jesus was probably not even buried. What about Jewish exceptions? What about the burial of crucified bodies before sunset? In Deuteronomy 21:22-23, there is the command, "When someone is convicted of a crime punishable by death and is executed and you hang him on a tree, his corpse must not remain all night upon the tree; because you shall bury him that same day." Notice, by the way, that the presumption is that you have already executed this person when you hang him on a tree, and you're hanging him as a warning. He is already dead; therefore, it is relatively easy to take him down by nightfall.

We know from the Temple Scroll, the longest of the Dead Sea Scrolls, that the Essenes talked about this; when they imagined that they would take over Jerusalem, they applied that text specifically to crucifixion. Not only when you kill somebody and hang him on a cross or a tree, but also when you hang him up to die, he must be buried on the same day. The question, however, is, to put it crudely, did Pilate read the Temple Scroll? Did Pilate care? Did the Romans observe Jewish piety?

There are two problems here. Everything we know about Pilate from outside the New Testament puts him on a collision course with Jewish religious sensibilities. Furthermore, when the Essenes tell us in the Temple Scroll what they want to do when they take over Jerusalem, they're probably telling us what's not being done right now. So the best hope we could have is that maybe, maybe, as an exception to standard Roman practice, Jesus was buried out of Jewish piety.

Textually and archaeologically, we do know this. Crucified bodies could be given to their families. Philo mentions this in his work *Against Flaccus* (81-84). He says, "I have known cases when on the eve of a holiday of this kind [birthdays of the illustrious Augustan house], people who have been crucified have been taken down and their bodies delivered to their kinsfolk." Then, in 1968 at Giv'at ha-Mivtar in northwest Jerusalem, the first crucified body was found and, in the same tomb complex, by the way, a man who had been burned alive and whose leg bones still showed the striations of the grid marks.

It was possible, therefore, for somebody to be buried by the family after being crucified. But remember that, in general, if you had power, you were not crucified. If you were crucified, you did not have the power to control your burial. According to Roman practices, then, Jesus would not be buried. For Jewish exceptions, *maybe* it is possible that Jewish piety was observed and Jesus was buried by the soldiers who crucified him.

But now I come to the third point, what I call Christian apologetics, that is, the steady improvement in Jesus' burial across the gospel texts. That's what makes me deeply suspicious about what was there at the beginning. Try and imagine if Jesus' followers had fled. They would not know what had happened, but they would know what happened to crucified people. What was their best hope? What was their worst fear?

In the Gospel of Peter (5:15-6:22), which I mentioned before, in a section I consider to be independent of the New Testament, there is an explicit reference to Deuteronomy, which presumes that Jesus would have been buried out of Jewish piety by those who had crucified him. They would at least have followed Deuteronomy and so, of course, he was buried. You can almost feel their hope and their fear in reading that text. Of course he was buried. He must have been buried. Somebody would have observed Deuteronomy. Notice that in the Gospel of Peter there's no talk of his being buried by his friends. In the Gospel of Peter, Jesus is buried by his enemies because of Deuteronomy 21:22-23.

We move on to Mark 15:42-47. We now have burial by a friend, but a somewhat inadequate one. "When evening had come, and since it was the Day of Preparation," that is, the day before the Sabbath, "Joseph of Arimathea, a respected member of the council who was also himself waiting expectantly for the kingdom of God, went boldly to Pilate and asked for the body of Jesus." That explains it. How could he have power and still be on Jesus' side? Well, he was a respected member of the council, so he was in the leading Jewish circles, but he was also looking for the kingdom of God. That explains everything plausibly. But, in case you have any doubts, we give you his name.

Matthew and Luke, who are the most careful readers that Mark ever got, notice this problem. Matthew decides not to mention the council. He simply says in 27:57, "There came a rich man from Arimathea, named Joseph, who also was a disciple of Jesus." That's one obvious solution to Mark's problematic conjunction of political power or access to Pilate *and* faith or sympathy for Jesus. Luke changes it in the equally obvious but opposite direction. He was a "member of the council," he says in 23:50-51, but, "a good and righteous man...who...had not agreed to their plan and action...he was waiting expectantly for the kingdom of God." That solves the Markan dilemma.

Finally, in John 19:38-42, this process reaches its climax. Jesus receives a regal burial by his friends. John has both Joseph of Arimathea (from Mark) and Nicodemus (from John 3:1-9, 7:50) involved together. "Nicodemus, who had at first come to Jesus by night, also came, bringing a mixture of myrrh and aloes, weighing about a hundred pounds." Jesus is now given what can only be described as a royal embalming. At the start, as history's real terror, were Jesus' enemies and the dogs. At the end, as faith's unreal apologetics, were his friends and the spices.

But no amount of damage control can conceal what this intensity confirms. With regard to the body of Jesus, by Easter Sunday morning, anyone who cared did not know where it was, and anyone who knew did not care. Why should the soldiers, even if they had given him a quick burial and gone home, remember the death and disposal of a nobody? Still, Matthew 27:19 records that Pilate's wife had troubled dreams that night. That never happened, of course, but it was true nonetheless. It was a propitious time for Roman imperialism to start having nightmares.

The Resurrection of Jesus. My third subject is the resurrection. I'll be dealing with three theses here. The first thesis is that resurrection was *one way, but only one way*, Jesus' earliest followers, after his execution, explained the continuation rather than the termination, the expansion rather than the contraction, of faith in Jesus as the manifestation of God.

Imagine some of these people from the Q community that Steve Patterson talked about three months after Jesus' execution. They are a couple. They are missionaries of the kingdom. They have been going out since they first met Jesus and doing what he told them to do. Dressed like destitute wanderers, they go into the rural hamlets bringing healing and eating with those they healed. They stay away from the big cities; they stay away from the market towns; they go to small, tiny hamlets, with 150 or 200 people. They go down the alleyways, and they enter a courtyard house. The homes around it are single rooms. Maybe an extended family, but maybe strangers share the courtyard. And they talk about the kingdom of God.

And then, three months after the execution of Jesus, they hear a rumor. They killed him. They executed him in Jerusalem. It takes another month before it's definite. They now have to explain something to themselves. How was it that for the last three months the divine empowerment wasn't turned off? How was it that the kingdom of God still seemed to be proceeding as well as it ever proceeded? They were still having some people believe and some people tell them to get out of here. And nothing changed three months ago when something was supposed to have happened to Jesus in Jerusalem. They never had an Easter Sunday. They never lost their faith. Jesus, after all, had warned them that wisdom would be rejected. It's a dangerous business we're in. Remember John the Baptist. It can happen to us. They are sad, extremely sad, of course, that Jesus is dead. But, get on with it. Get on with it.

Imagine another case. Imagine Paul in 1 Corinthians 15, which everyone quotes because it has become normative, as if this were the only type of Christianity in the first century. Paul concludes in 1 Corinthians 15:13,16 that, "If there is no resurrection of the dead, then Christ has not been raised....For if the dead are not raised, then Christ has not been raised."

Why does he argue it that way? Why, even if there is no *general* resurrection, can't Christ be raised anyhow? What Paul is saying is this: I am a Pharisee, and I believe in the general resurrection. As far as I am concerned, Jesus has risen from the dead, and is, according to 15:20, "the first fruits of those that have died." The resurrection of Jesus starts, in other words, the general resurrection, just as the first fruits start the general harvest. For Paul, the harvest has begun; the resurrection of the dead has begun.

We usually say that Paul expected the end of the world soon. That, I think, is flatly wrong. Paul considered that the end of the world *had already begun*, and only by the mercy of God was it holding until Paul and others could get around widely enough among the gentiles to warn them. That's the way I see Paul. His logic is quite clear. General resurrection and Jesus' resurrection stand or fall together. The general resurrection has begun. And, he insists, if this is wrong, then our preaching is in vain.

But does Paul speak for all of early Christianity? That is the question I want to ask. The people of the Q gospel don't think like that. If you were to talk to the people of the Q gospel and ask them if Jesus was risen from the dead, they would probably reply that such was not their language. If you asked them where Jesus is, they might have answered that he is with God. "What do you mean by that?" "We don't know. All we know is that the empowerment of Jesus is still operative in our lives." "Is he risen?" "Well, if that's your language, okay, but it's not ours."

It is Paul's language, however, and I don't think Paul could put it any other way. I wouldn't know how to interpret Paul except within the framework of his belief that the general resurrection has begun. Resurrection is crucial for Paul.

But should we take Paul's language and make it normative for all of early Christianity? My thesis is that there were other types of Christians in the first century who did not confess Jesus using the term resurrection. They might, for example, as in the Gospel of Thomas, speak about "the living Jesus." And if you said, "Do you mean the risen Jesus?" They might reply, "No, the living Jesus. Yesterday, today, tomorrow and forever. What do you mean, risen? That's not the way we think."

I now move from my first to my second thesis. Paul had experienced Jesus. Paul had a vision. Paul had a revelation. And he must equate that experience with the experience of Jesus' earliest followers. Otherwise his own authority is at stake. He mentions, as you know, in 1 Corinthians 15:1-8, the appearances of the risen Jesus. He appeared to Cephas, to the Twelve, to more than 500 people, to James, to all the apostles and last of all to Paul himself. A vision of the risen Lord was determinative for Paul. And he, I think for rather obvious political reasons, says it's determinative for everyone. It is the vision of the risen Lord that makes *him* an apostle on a par with the others.

My third and final thesis is this. Risen apparitions after the execution are not at all about the origins of Christian *faith* but about the origins of Christian *authority*. They are not about belief but about power within those early communities. And I do not really say that pejoratively. I'm simply trying to describe what these texts are interested in.

Let me give you an example. In Luke 24:12, to exalt Peter as the leader, you have the following episode: "But Peter got up and ran to the tomb; stooping and looking in, he saw the linen cloths by themselves; then he went home, amazed at what had happened." The women have announced the empty tomb, but Peter is the only one who runs to the tomb. The emphasis on Peter is clear. But supposing *in your community* you didn't believe that Peter really was that important. What could you do with that piece of tradition?

Let me read what John 20:3-10 does with it. What he intends to do is exalt his own Beloved Disciple (the "other disciple") over Peter. (1) "Then Peter and the other disciple set out and went toward the tomb. The two were running together, but the other disciple outran Peter and reached the tomb first. (2) He bent down to look in and he saw the linen wrappings lying there, but he did not go in. (3) Then Simon Peter came, following him, and went into the tomb. He saw the linen wrappings lying there and the cloth that had been on Jesus' head, not lying with the linen wrappings but rolled up in a place by itself." Now we come to the clincher in point four. The Beloved Disciple got there first and looked in first, but Peter went in first. (4) "Then the other disciple, who reached the tomb first, also went in and *he* saw and *he* believed" (italics added). It doesn't say that Peter didn't believe, but it doesn't say that *they* believed either. It says *he* saw and *he* believed. Then the story reverts to the plural. (5) "For as yet they did not understand the scripture, that he must rise from the dead. Then the disciples returned to their homes."

I can see only one way of understanding that apostolic race to the tomb. To Luke, Peter is the leader, so Peter is the only one who gets to run to the tomb. For John, the Beloved Disciple cannot quite ignore that tradition about Peter's authority. But the Beloved Disciple does everything important. He gets there first, he looks in first and, above all, *he* believes.

Suppose, now, that you wanted to come back from the Peter side with a counter-exaltation of Peter. Look at John 21:9: "When they [Peter and six other disciples] had gone ashore, they saw a charcoal fire there, with fish on it." Why a charcoal fire? The last time we saw a charcoal fire was when Peter, around the charcoal fire, denied Jesus three times in John (18:17,25,27).

Watch what happens. Jesus said to Simon Peter, " 'Simon son of John, do you love me more than these [the other apostles]?' He said to him, 'Yes, Lord; you know that I love you.' Jesus said to him, 'Feed my lambs.' A second time he said to him, 'Simon son of John, do you love me?' He said to him, 'Yes, Lord; you know that I love you.' Jesus said to him, 'Tend my sheep.'" Even though *lambs* and *sheep* should exhaust the possibilities, you need a third time. Peter denied Jesus three times, so he had to affirm Jesus three times. "He said to him the third time, 'Simon son of John, do you love me?' Peter felt hurt because he said to him the third time, 'Do you love me?' And he said to him, 'Lord, you know everything; you know that I love you.' Jesus said to him, 'Feed my sheep.'" The sheep must be repeated to fill out the required threesome.

Peter wins out. It seems to me absolutely clear that what people are doing in these stories is trying to decide who's in charge in the various communities. And the way you decide that is by claiming who saw Jesus. To whom did Jesus speak?

In conclusion, Christian faith is faith in the historical Jesus *as* the manifestation of God. Resurrection is one way, but only one way, of expressing the absence as presence, or presence despite absence, of Jesus as experienced in the world by a believer. Leaving aside Paul, whose experience was exactly what Marcus Borg was talking about earlier, an experience of an altered state of consciousness, a vision of Jesus, the other experiences in the last chapters of our New Testament Gospels are not intended to be visions or hallucinations or anything else in that sense. They are calm, serene statements of who is in charge in this community and who is in charge in that other community.

ENDNOTES

1. John Dominic Crossan, *The Cross That Spoke: The Origins of the Passion Narrative* (San Francisco: Harper & Row, 1988).

2. Martin Hengel, *Crucifixion in the Ancient World and the Folly of the Message of the Cross* (Philadelphia: Fortress, 1977), pp. 86-88.

QUESTIONS & ANSWERS

Thank you for an inspiring and uplifting talk, which brings to mind a book that was prominent in England called *Holy Blood, Holy Grail* (Dell, 1983) by three British authors. It was sensational at the time it was published. The book takes the position that Christ was not crucified but that an arrangement was made under which Christ was taken away, not crucified, just taken away, and that Christ led a normal life, including marriage. My question to you, sir, is this. Can you comment on this book, which was, incidentally, highly criticized by the Church of England?

I don't believe a single word of it. I haven't read the book, but I have heard of it. I would consider that the crucifixion of Jesus is as historically certain as anything in the world can ever be. Because, as we said, it's in Tacitus, it's in Josephus and it's in the Christian writings. And it was a terrible embarrassment. I do not see any evidence whatsoever to prove that Jesus survived his crucifixion physically. I think, actually, if you try to face what crucifixion was, it's sensational enough just by itself. It doesn't have to be sensationalized.

I think you have enunciated a male point of view. It was Mary Magdalene who got to the tomb first, and she was the first person to recognize Jesus.

In Mark's Gospel, which is the earliest of the Gospels, Mary and the women get to the tomb first. This is part of Mark's polemic against the family of Jesus and the disciples. The women don't tell anyone; they run away. I would not put much on that, in itself.

What I would emphasize are two other points. First, in John 20 he takes Peter and sort of debunks him. At the end, he takes on Thomas, the traditions that the Gospel of Thomas is based on, and debunks him. But in the middle, he goes after Mary Magdalene. In John, she keeps getting it wrong. She says three times, in 20:2,13,15, "They've stolen the body." In terms of the Johannine community, Peter, Mary Magdalene and Thomas are important leaders who all need to be downgraded. Second, if I wanted to find a woman to exalt, I would follow exactly the story in Mark 14:3-9. I would emphasize the unnamed woman who alone believes in Jesus, anoints him because she knows if she doesn't anoint him now, she's never going to get a chance again.

She's the only one who believes in Jesus. The disciples have been told repeatedly in Mark, "I'm going to die and rise, I'm going to die and rise," and they say, "Yeah, yeah, yeah." This woman believes it. She's unnamed, and we're told that, in memory of her, this story is going to be told whenever the gospel is told, something that's said of nothing else. If I was looking for an ideal female Christian hero, she's the one I would claim because she is the first one who comes to faith. And notice she comes to faith before Easter.

I would like to know how the Word in the New Testament was handed down, and in what sort of gathering it was discussed. If there was no written word left for us to follow, in what setting was it that the Word was talked about and handed down as far as the New Testament is concerned?

I think we have to look at two different tracks, very distinct, and they're separated according to class. When Jesus was a peasant talking to peasants, anyone who had the courage could live like Jesus. And he told them, "You too can bring the kingdom. I don't have a monopoly on it." All it meant was adopting a lifestyle like Jesus'. That couple I talked about, the one wandering through the alleys preaching the kingdom, knew that Jesus had said don't wear shoes, not because their memories were good, but because their feet were very sore. In other words, it's in the continuation of a lifestyle like Jesus' that the real guaranteed continuity between Jesus and the earliest Christians is found. It's not in their memories at all. It's in their lifestyle. If they remember what he said, it's just to justify their lifestyle. In one way you could say the continuity is in mimesis or imitation, not in memory. Now that's one group, and that could be practiced by anyone with courage.

There were obviously other groups who also heard Jesus, like people in the retainer class that Marcus Borg talked about earlier. They were operating in Jerusalem and were searching the Hebrew Scriptures. To search the Scriptures, they had to be able to read. Those people were going through and looking for texts to apply to Jesus. I think they were a different social class. Both those tracks were operating at a very early stage. I find much more continuity in the words than I find in the deeds, because most of the deeds are creating history to suit prophecy. They are creating, actually, most of the narrative material, as distinct from the sayings material. So you have different kinds of continuities. In a way, the words and the deeds of Jesus operate on different principles and in different social classes.

Three questions: From the discussion it appears that you do not assume that Matthew is written by the apostle but by somebody else. And I'm wondering who you assume wrote Matthew. Number two: Why would the Christians put into the account the story of Peter's denial three times? And three: How would you interpret the words of Christ from the cross, "Why hast thou forsaken me"? That sounds much more like that would be historical. I can't see how that would aid the Christians.

Let me go back to something crucial that Steve Patterson said earlier. Mark is followed by Matthew and Luke. They use Mark's passion account as a source. So if you have all three of them doing anything, you still have only one independent source. Second, is John an independent source? I don't believe it with regard to the passion account. I can't find anything distinctive there.

So we have to watch Mark very carefully. Does it make sense for Mark to insist that Peter is a jerk, to put it bluntly? Yes, for Mark. No, for Matthew. Does it make sense to say that one of the Twelve betrayed him? For Mark, yes. Does it make sense for Mark to say that on the cross Jesus is abandoned? Yes, because Mark's going to have no apparitions. He's writing for a persecuted community who should *not* believe that Jesus appears, because he didn't appear when they needed him. He is trying to prepare them for the period between the death of Jesus and the Parousia [the second coming]. Jesus felt abandoned by God—so will you. This is the terrible lost loneliness. Jesus felt it and you should be ready for it. Mark is talking to people who are being persecuted, and apparitions don't work for them. You can't tell people, "Don't worry, God will intervene," when they're really being persecuted.

I think Mark comes out of a situation of real persecution, and you have to be very careful to understand what Mark is doing. So, yes, for Mark to say, "My God, my God, why hast thou forsaken me," makes sense for Mark. That's the way his people felt when they were being killed. That's the way most people feel, if they get to think about it, when they're being killed. Abandoned. So he is trying to speak to them with Jesus' death as their model. But remember, that's Mark.

Even that example, isn't that simply a quotation from Psalm 22, and couldn't that quotation simply be another instance of prophecy historicized?

Yes, I presume it is. But you get to choose. In a certain sense, all prophecy is there to choose from. You can highlight that. For example, compare the death of Jesus in Mark with the death of Jesus in John. You don't get anything in John about, "My God, my God, why hast thou forsaken me." Jesus dies in John when he's good and ready. He asks for a drink to fulfill the Scriptures, and he dies when he is ready. In Mark, he dies in agony. In John, he dies in triumph. Those are different ways of choosing what to use.

I have no problem with your central thesis, that a lot of the passion narratives are prophecy historicized. But my question is why one would bother to do that in the first place unless one is thoroughly convinced that one had been in the presence of the Divine. And wouldn't it take something like

the appearance of a resurrected figure to get one to go through the exercise, in the first place, of constructing a narrative that would convince others that prophesies had been fulfilled?

My answer is flatly no. Let me recall the term Marcus Borg used—spirit person. In every great religion, some people have ecstatic experiences. I don't think Ghandi ever had one, but I do think Ghandi is a religious figure. There are different ways that people experience the Divine. Some go through this sort of magnificent mystical experience. For other people, the Divine is so obvious that they do not have mystical experiences. I think for Paul it took an ecstatic vision. I do not think that was necessary for everyone. It trivializes Christianity to say it took a vision to jar everyone back to where some had always remained. My thesis, remember, is that Christian faith was not Easter faith. It was there as soon as anyone saw God in Jesus. And there were people whose faith was strong enough that God was still in Jesus without worrying about his execution. I think that's true to human nature. It does not always take visions. There are also people who don't give up.

Some people, the elites, went back to the Scriptures. I'm not sure at all that the Q-types, if they could read, would have been impressed one way or the other. They knew the kingdom was working because it was working. Nothing had changed. It wasn't better or worse. They were experiencing it in ordinary, everyday life. I consider that as much an experience of God as Paul being knocked to the ground with a blinding-light-type revelation. There are different kinds of revelation. Not better or worse, just different.

VI. PANEL DISCUSSION

Hershel Shanks: A couple of questions have been raised to me by people in the audience, and I am going to pass them on as the first questions from the audience.

One of the requests was that we give more dates. We talked a lot about Mark and the date of Mark's Gospel, around the time of the First Jewish Revolt (66-70 C.E.). But what about Matthew and Luke? And in what circumstances were they composed?

Dom Crossan: It is important that you understand the difference between dating when a manuscript was copied and dating when the contents were composed. You can say, more or less objectively, that this manuscript was written in the year 200. And that's about when you get a first copy of Matthew and Luke. That's objective. If you ask when the text was first composed, not this copy, but when the original content was composed, where it was composed, by whom, that all has to be interpreted from within the text. And therefore it is open to debate. For example, 85 is the standard date, around 85 for Matthew. Where? Well, everyone says Antioch. Antioch must have been crowded with people writing Christian documents. I mean, we're always looking for big cities. We're looking for Rome, Antioch, Alexandria.

Marcus Borg: I have nothing to add to that except that Luke is most commonly put in that same time frame, roughly around 85 or 90. A few people argue that Luke-Acts is much later, but I don't think they reflect the majority position. So roughly around 90 for both of them is the common wisdom I hear.

Shanks: Dom, you used the word *parousia* without defining it.

Crossan: *Parousia* simply means presence. It's the coming of a king to his country, as it were. It's used to mean the return of Jesus, the second coming, the end of the world, with the scenario left magnificently vague, but with certainty that everything is going to be really different after that. We, the good people, are going to be triumphant, and you, whoever you are, the bad people, are really going to get it. I think of it, to be blunt with you, as divine ethnic cleansing.

Shanks: Steve, you spoke of Josephus' testimony. How do we know that Jesus even existed? Some people doubt his existence. You spoke of not only New Testament testimonies and witnesses, but also of Josephus, and, I believe, you mentioned the Talmud. The question that has been raised is that these extra-New Testament witnesses are not entirely reliable. Would you comment on that?

Steve Patterson: I would just say that none of these texts is any closer chronologically, historically, or socially to Jesus of Nazareth than our Gospels. So in this sense, they certainly are no more reliable sources of information than the Gospels. But since scholars normally regard the Christian Gospels as theologically tendentious, they are almost universally rejected as reliable historical sources in scholarly circles. And so it's helpful to try to shore up at least a few basic points using other secular historians who are not so committed to the Christian cause. But as you rightly point out, these historians are not historians in the modern sense. As ancient persons, they have no more modern historical sensibility than Matthew, Mark, Luke or John. So, while secular historians are helpful in establishing basic facts such as the historical existence of Jesus, we should not feel overly confident about the few facts they might give us about Jesus' life.

Shanks: Isn't the Josephus text you read from the *Testimonium Flavianum*? From Flavius Josephus? Isn't that regarded as a late Christian interpolation into Josephus?

Patterson: The text I read from Josephus' work *The Antiquities of the Jews* is not entirely a Christian interpolation. There are parts of it, however, that are almost universally recognized as Christian interpolations. You must remember that all of these texts, whether by Josephus or Roman historians or Greek historians, all of them were preserved by Christians. That is, they were all passed along from antiquity to the modern period through the Christian monastic tradition of copying and preserving manuscripts. Since the hand copying of manuscripts is an imprecise process, very few ancient manuscripts managed to survive antiquity without corruption. And Josephus, of course, is a good example of that. There are many, many Christian interpolations in Josephus, places where Josephus' words are amended to reflect a Christian perspective. The text that I read to you this morning has several such interpolations; however, I took the liberty of purging them as I read.

Shanks: Is this Josephus text an example of a text that's been tampered with? We're not talking about biblical texts now but other kinds of texts. Can't this passage from Josephus serve as an example that the same kind of thing happened in the transmission of biblical texts?

Patterson: Yes, we have the same problem with biblical manuscripts. The Greek New Testament, the text that scholars use in their work and the text upon which all modern translations are based, does not actually exist in antiquity. It is a critical reconstruction, that is, a conglomeration of and a melding of the best readings of literally hundreds of ancient manuscripts, no single one of which is flawless. That is to say, every manuscript from antiquity has errors, usually lots of errors. The first job of a biblical scholar is to go through all of these manuscripts and, by a process of comparison, weed out as many of these errors as possible in an effort to come up with a text, a critically reconstructed text or a conglomerate text, if you will, that is as free of late emendations and tampering as possible. This sort of work must be done across the board on all ancient texts. None of them, not even the best biblical manuscripts, has been handed down to us error free, and it is the first job of scholars to come up with a text that stands as close to the original autograph as possible.

Could you very briefly recap where the gospel authors came from? Not location, but did any of them know Jesus? Who did they know? Who were they writing for? You know, what was their general purpose? Mark, Matthew, Luke, Thomas, John and Paul. I mean, just one sentence.

Borg: I'm leaving Paul off the list for the moment. About the others, we don't know anything at all about who they were. With almost complete certainty, we can say they did not bear the names by which the gospels are known. None of them knew Jesus while he was alive. They weren't the 12 disciples. That is, John wasn't written by one of the Twelve; Matthew wasn't written by one of the Twelve. So in that sense, they are all anonymous documents. I think it's also safe to say that they were all written for Christian communities and not really for the larger world. That is, they are in-house documents for a worshiping community.

Shanks: To what audience were they addressed? We often hear of the Johannine community or the Lukan community or Matthean community. Are those hypothetical? Or can we say anything specific about the audiences to which the canonical Gospels and Thomas and Q were addressed?

Patterson: I will speak to that. But first I want to add just one more thing about the authors themselves. The fact that they could write means that they belonged to the very upper stratum of Greek and Roman and Jewish society. This is indicated by the mere fact that they were literate. So few people were literate in the ancient world, this would have separated the gospel writers from the vast majority of Christians. So one of the things that sometimes troubles me is that we have in the written legacy of ancient Christianity something that is not the product, or at least not the direct product, of most Christians living in antiquity. It is the product of a very small, elite group within that community. I think we have to take that into consideration when we read these documents.

I do think, however, that these authors were writing for communities, presumably communities in which they lived. And these texts would have normally been read aloud to people. So that the experience of a gospel for an ancient Christian would normally have been an oral experience, that is, they heard a gospel read to them. This implies, of course, that the relationship between author and audience was much more intimate than can be assumed for most literature today.

Who were the communities for whom these texts were written? What were these communities like? The Johannine community is probably one that we would consider relatively sectarian. It perceives itself as being persecuted. It has probably been in conflict with the larger Jewish community. It is a Jewish community, perhaps a Jewish gentile community, but it perceives itself as having been cast out of the larger Jewish community and, for that reason, has sort of hunkered down for the long haul. The Gospel itself promises this community the presence of the spirit of Jesus for comfort in this time of turmoil and trouble. Let me defer to the others for the other gospels.

Crossan: The result of this would be that we have to face an intense pluralism as far back as we can go in the history of the Christian movement.

We've been talking about the historical Jesus and, by inference, the religion that evolved as a result of his life. But I'm wondering if you would comment on what that religion might be like today if Paul had never come on the scene.

Crossan: It's very important to take class or, if you prefer, where you are in the pecking order, into account. Before Paul, apart from Paul, there were already at least two elements we can distinguish—the type of people we talked about in connection with the Q gospel or the early Thomas movement, both of whom could well be peasants. That element required no one to search the scriptures to see if Jesus could be the Elect One of God.

But there was also a second element, followers of Jesus who were learned, and they're before Paul. As far as I can see, they were there from the beginning, and they're connected with Jerusalem. So I imagine in Galilee and Syria, in that area, there were people who continued the lifestyle of Jesus. I don't mean they were only peasants, but you could be in that wing of the movement even if you were a peasant. If you were in Jerusalem searching the Scriptures, you could not participate fully unless you could read. But that was also there before Paul. So already, the peasants and the retainers were starting to take over. Paul is just one more retainer. But there were retainers before him.

Borg: The beginning of a gentile mission was there before Paul, so that can't be ascribed simply to Paul. But trying to imagine Christianity without the Pauline epistles and the effect the Pauline epistles have had is very interesting. It means that a lot of vocabulary that's common in the Christian church would certainly not be there. For example, language that has been particularly important in the Protestant tradition— justification, sanctification and so forth. We simply wouldn't use that language. Whether we might still talk about those things in different words, I think, is quite possible.

Patterson: I thought I detected in the question a somewhat pejorative tone relative to Paul. Paul is often given a rather rough shake today in enlightened circles. There are many reasons for this. Often, it is because people fail to distinguish critically between Paul's authentic letters and letters that were attributed to Paul later, which he did not in fact write, such as, for example, the pastoral epistles—1 and 2 Timothy and Titus. In those epistles, we find some of the most problematic things for people to accept, especially in terms of women and women's roles in the church today.

But I think Paul, for all his faults, did have some important insights. And one of them has to do with the implications of Jesus' preaching for community life. Paul insisted that for communities to be authentically Christian they must be mixed groups; in particular, they must be communities that include both Jews and gentiles. Now, you have to understand that this meant Paul's churches had to include people from two sides of a very tumultuous and contested social boundary. Paul insisted that the social implications, the communal implications, of the gospel meant that people had to learn to live together in diverse, tolerant communities. And I think that's one of the most important insights of the early Christian movement. Without Paul, we may not have had that so clearly expressed.

Crossan: Could I add one thing to that? I asked you to imagine early Christianity before Paul. Imagine Paul before Lutheranism. In Rome, what was important was not Paul, but Peter and Paul. Peter and Paul, always together and always in that order. You had Romulus and Remus, the hero twins of the empire. Now we have our hero twins, Peter and Paul. We talk about them as martyrs. We don't mention that Paul wrote letters. We're not too certain we can even handle it. But they're martyrs, and they're a pair, and they're a pair in that order. That's very important, I think, to understanding how Paul became important before Protestantism.

Borg: When I was teaching in a Protestant ecumenical seminary a few years ago, I had Catholic students as well as Protestant students in my class. We got to Paul, and about two-thirds of the class was talking about justification by grace. Finally, one of the Catholic students raised her hand and said, "What's justification? I have never heard of the word." That's a way of underlining how Paul has been highlighted by the effect of the Protestant Reformation on Christianity.

Harold Bloom, the literary critic, didn't make a lot of friends among biblical scholars with his introduction to *The Book of J* (Random House, 1991). But he made an interesting observation that I'd like to comment on. He says that, in so many religions, first there's a visionary who creates or receives the message of the religion, and then there's a bureaucrat who

puts it into practice. In the United States, for instance, we had Joseph Smith, the visionary, and then Brigham Young was, say, the first CEO, of Salt Lake City. In the case of the New Testament, we have Jesus, the visionary, and then Paul, the one who formulates rules and helps put the faith into practice. Would you say something about this?

Borg: Bloom is using a distinction that comes from Abraham Maslow at this point. And it's an interesting distinction. Maslow wrote about peak experiences, which most of you have heard of. Maslow makes the very interesting, but a little bit lopsided, observation that religions are founded by people who have peak experiences, and they are sustained by non-peakers, that is, by bureaucrats who don't have peak experiences. If you don't have peak experiences, you think that what the religion is about is the words rather than what the words say. In early Christianity, though, I don't think I would speak of Jesus as the visionary and Paul as the bureaucrat or the codifier. If we want to look for people who fit into that category, let me pick my favorite whipping boy in the New Testament. It would be the author of Matthew's Gospel. I think among the Gospels, Matthew seems to be moving more in the direction of a kind of conventional wisdom and a concern with church order. So I think that process is going on in early Christianity, but I wouldn't see Jesus and Paul as the central figures in that contrast.

I thought I heard Dom say about the virgin birth that he believed that James could be Jesus' elder brother. I'm not here to draw lines between Protestantism and Catholicism, but I do know this. Without the virgin birth, if Jesus was

blemished, I can hang on a cross for everybody in here and it does nobody any good. There's no eternal life. I'm not here to critique anybody, but I couldn't keep my mouth shut.

Crossan: I think what I would say to that is you have to listen to the other people in the audience.

Borg: I'll comment briefly on the connection between a literal or biological virgin birth and Jesus being free of blemish. The idea is that only if he's free of blemish can he be an adequate sacrifice for sin. That's the logic of part of your comment. I would simply note that the image of Jesus as free from sin, free from blemish, is really something that goes along with the metaphor or the image of Jesus as the Lamb of God who dies for the sins of the world. A sacrificial lamb had to be without blemish, therefore it gets attached to Jesus. Later in the tradition, the virgin birth is explained on these grounds: "Well that's how he could be without sin."

What's going on here is the literalizing of a metaphor. The metaphor is very, very powerful as a metaphor. To say that Jesus is the Lamb of God who takes away the sins of the world is to say there is nothing that separates us from God except our own sense of unworthiness. Everything's been taken care of, is the meaning of that metaphor. When the metaphor is literalized, I think, it gets inappropriately tied up with the conception of Jesus.

Patterson: I would like to add to that. I think that what we have said this afternoon and this morning in terms of history, especially the negative conclusions we have come to, is often difficult for people with strong religious convictions to accept because in our culture we associate truth so closely with historical accuracy and reliability with historical facticity. I would simply like to remind you that that is a modern sensibility. People in the ancient world seem to have no concern about that at all. They do not share our assumptions. And so when one looks at the Gospel of Mark and reads it as though it were a factual report, and if, at the same time, one assumes that it has no validity unless it is factual, then you are insisting on reading that Gospel in your own terms instead of the terms in which Mark originally wrote it. It is your prerogative to do that, but you should not assume the universal validity of your perspective.

But you should understand that, when we analyze these texts historically, we are not assuming that their validity rests upon historical reliability. We are simply trying to understand these texts in the terms in which they were originally written. And that means we cannot bring to them a modern sort of historical agenda or try to recast them and make them into something we wish they were rather than what they are. So I would remind you that just because we call the virgin birth mythic or fictional...and I would concur with Dom that the virgin birth is not an historical fact...does not mean that I do not believe what the virgin birth seems to be saying.

The story of the virgin birth is the story of the birth of a god. It is Luke's way of saying that in Jesus we have encountered the face of God. And that is a faith claim. It asks one to put one's chips with Jesus. The risk involved in that cannot be minimized by historical investigation. That is, I can affirm what Luke is saying without having to embrace the ancient idiom he uses to express that claim. In other words, you don't have to adopt an ancient idiom as literally true in order to profess Christian faith in the 20th century.

Shanks: And that's an excellent place to end, in a wonderful spirit. You've been a wonderful audience, and your participation has been buoying and sustaining for us. Thank you indeed.

■ BIBLIOGRAPHY AND RELATED READINGS ■

Borg, Marcus J. *Conflict, Holiness and Politics in the Teachings of Jesus* (Lewiston, NY: Edwin Mellen Press, 1984).

———. *Jesus, A New Vision: Spirit, Culture, and the Life of Discipleship* (San Francisco: Harper & Row, 1987).

———. "Portraits of Jesus in Contemporary North American Scholarship," *Harvard Theological Review* 84 (1991).

———. *Meeting Jesus Again for the First Time* (HarperSanFrancisco, 1994).

———. *Jesus in Contemporary Scholarship* (Philadelphia: Trinity Press International, forthcoming).

Brueggemann, Walter. *The Bible Makes Sense* (Atlanta: John Knox, 1977).

Celsus. *On the True Doctrine*, trans. R. Joseph Hoffman (New York: Oxford University Press, 1987).

Crossan, John Dominic. "From Moses to Jesus: Parallel Themes," *Bible Review* 2:2 (1986).

———. *The Cross That Spoke: The Origins of the Passion Narrative* (San Francisco: Harper & Row, 1988).

———. "Materials and Methods in Historical Jesus Research," *Forum* 4:4 (1988).

———. *The Historical Jesus: The Life of a Mediterranean Jewish Peasant* (HarperSanFrancisco, 1992).

———. *Jesus: A Revolutionary Biography* (HarperSanFrancisco, 1994).

Danker, Frederick W. *Benefactor: Epigraphic Study of a Graeco-Roman and New Testament Semantic Field* (St. Louis: Clayton Publishing House, 1982).

Funk, Robert W., Roy Hoover and the Jesus Seminar. *The Five Gospels: The Search for the Authentic Words of Jesus* (New York: Macmillan, 1993).

Griesbach, Johann-Jakob. *Synopsis evangeliorum Matthaei, Marci, et Lucae* (Halle, 1776).

———. *Commentatio qua Marci evangelium totum e Matthaei et Lucae commentariis decerptum esse monstratur* (Jena, 1789-90).

Harris, William V. *Ancient Literacy* (Cambridge, MA: Harvard University Press, 1989).

Hartley, Leslie P. *The Go-Between* (New York: Stein and Day, 1953).

Hengel, Martin. *Crucifixion in the Ancient World and the Folly of the Message of the Cross* (Philadelphia: Fortress, 1977).

Holtzmann, Heinrich Julius. *Die synoptischen Evangelien* (Leipzig: Wilhelm Engelmann, 1863).

Horsley, Richard. *Jesus and the Spiral of Violence* (San Francisco: Harper & Row, 1987).

———. *The Liberation of Christmas* (New York: Crossroad, 1989).

———. *Sociology and the Jesus Movement* (New York: Crossroad, 1989).

Horsley, Richard, and John S. Hanson. *Bandits, Prophets, and Messiahs* (Minneapolis: Winston, 1985).

Jacobson, Arland. *The First Gospel: An Introduction to Q* (Sonoma, CA: Polebridge, 1992).

Kaehler, Martin. *The So-Called Historical Jesus and the Historic, Biblical Christ* (Philadelphia: Fortress, 1964).

Koester, Helmut. *Ancient Christian Gospels: Their History and Development* (Philadelphia: Trinity Press International, 1990).

Kloppenborg, John, Marvin Meyer, Stephen Patterson and Michael Steinhauser. *The Q-Thomas Reader* (Sonoma, CA: Polebridge, 1990).

Lenski, Gerhard. *Power and Privilege: A Theory of Social Stratification* (New York: McGraw-Hill, 1966).

Lord, Albert. *The Singer of Tales* (Cambridge, MA: Harvard University Press, 1960).

Mack, Burton. *A Myth of Innocence: Mark and Christian Origins* (Philadelphia: Fortress, 1988).

————. *The Lost Gospel: The Book of Q and Christian Origins* (HarperSanFrancisco, 1993).

Malina, Bruce J. *The New Testament World: Insights from Cultural Anthropology*, rev. ed. (Louisville, KY: Westminster/John Knox, 1993).

Malina, Bruce J., and Richard Rohrbaugh. *Social Science Commentary on the Synoptic Gospels* (Minneapolis: Fortress, 1992).

Miller, Robert J., ed. *The Complete Gospels* (Sonoma, CA: Polebridge, 1992).

Niell, Stephen, and Tom Wright. *The Interpretation of the New Testament, 1861-1986*, 2d ed. (New York: Oxford University Press, 1988).

Ong, Walter. *Orality and Literacy* (New York: Methuen, 1982).

Orchard, Bernard B., and Thomas Longstaff, eds. *J. J. Griesbach: Synoptic and Critical Studies 1776-1976* (Cambridge, UK/New York: Cambridge University Press, 1978).

Pagels, Elaine. *The Gnostic Gospels* (New York: Random House, 1980).

Patterson, Stephen J. *The Gospel of Thomas and Jesus* (Sonoma, CA: Polebridge, 1993).

Robinson, James M. *A New Quest of the Historical Jesus (and Other Essays)* (Philadelphia: Fortress, 1983).

Sanders, E.P. *Jesus and Judaism* (Philadelphia: Fortress, 1985).

Sanders, E.P., and Margaret Davies. *Studying the Synoptic Gospels* (Philadelphia: Trinity Press International, 1989).

Schüssler Fiorenza, Elisabeth. *In Memory of Her: A Feminist Theological Reconstruction of Christian Origins* (New York: Crossroad, 1983).

Schweitzer, Albert. *The Quest of the Historical Jesus* (New York: Macmillan, 1961). German original published in 1906.

Tatum, W. Barnes. *In Quest of Jesus: A Guidebook* (Atlanta: John Knox, 1982).

Thiessen, Gerd. *The Shadow of the Galilean* (Philadelphia: Fortress, 1987).

Throckmorton, Burton H. *Gospel Parallels* (Toronto: Thomas Nelson, 1967).

Tuckett, Christopher M. *The Revival of the Griesbach Hypothesis* (Cambridge, UK/New York: Cambridge University Press, 1983).

Vermes, Geza. *Jesus the Jew: A Historian's Reading of the Gospels* (Philadelphia: Fortress, 1981).

———. *Jesus and the World of Judaism* (Philadelphia: Fortress, 1984).

———. *The Religion of Jesus the Jew* (Minneapolis: Fortress, 1993).

Weiss, Johannes. *Jesus' Proclamation of the Kingdom of God* (Philadelphia: Fortress, 1972). German original published in 1892.

Weisse, Christian Hermann. *Die evangelische Geschichte kritisch und philosophisch bearbeitet,* 2 vols. (Leipzig: Breitkopf und Hartel, 1838).

Wink, Walter. *Engaging the Powers* (Minneapolis: Fortress, 1992).

Wrede, William. *The Messianic Secret* (Cambridge, UK: J. Clarke, 1971). German original published in 1901.

■ ACKNOWLEDGMENTS ■

The BIBLICAL ARCHAEOLOGY SOCIETY is grateful to Carol Arenberg, Laurie Andrews, Judy Wohlberg, Sean O'Brien, Carla Murphy and Susan Laden for their devoted work preparing this book for publication.